D1188220

TWENTIETH CENTURY
PILGRIMAGE

CHARLES WELLBORN

TWENTIETH CENTURY PILGRIMAGE

Walter Lippmann and the Public Philosophy

LOUISIANA STATE UNIVERSITY PRESS
Baton Rouge

To my sons
Gary Marshall
Jon Richard

LIBRARY
FLORIDA STATE UNIVERSITY
TALLAHASSEE. FLORIDA

Copyright © 1969 by
LOUISIANA STATE UNIVERSITY PRESS

Library of Congress Catalog Card Number: 69–17624
SBN 8071–0303–9
Manufactured in the United States of America by
The Colonial Press Inc., Clinton, Massachusetts

Designed by Jules B. McKee

Acknowledgments

This volume has been in preparation over a period of four years. To acknowledge with any adequacy the help and influence of all who have contributed to such a project is an impossibility. The author himself is not consciously aware of many of the sources of ideas and concepts which have become a part of his personal intellectual equipment. It is a privilege, however, to express gratitude to some of those whose assistance has been more obvious.

My graduate professors at Duke University deserve my special appreciation. To three of them specific acknowledgment should be made. The original interest in the general area with which this volume concerns itself was stirred in Professor John H. Hallowell's classes in political theory, and his influence on my thinking will be clear to anyone familiar with Mr. Hallowell's work. Professor Creighton Lacy gave generously in time and counsel, and Professor Waldo Beach was a consistent source of encouragement.

I am indebted to the library staffs at Duke University, both in the General Library and in the Divinity School, for their assistance, and to the staff of the Historical Documents Sections of the Sterling Library at Yale University, who helped make my research in the Lippmann Collection convenient and worthwhile. Mr. Robert

Anthony, the honorary curator of the Lippmann Collection, was courteously helpful.

For material aid during the period in which this book was written I am indebted to the Cal-Tex Foundation of Houston, Texas, and to Mr. Joe W. Albritton for generous grants. Mr. Jack Jones of Arlington, Virginia, was also the donor of financial support. For the year 1963–64 I was the recipient of a fellowship grant from the Fund for Theological Education.

Mrs. C. C. Nelson, Jr., typed the original manuscript of the doctoral dissertation upon which this book is based. Mrs. Jean Blasberg, secretary par excellence, typed the final copies, assisted by Miss Barbara Mizell. And I owe much to the intellectual stimulation of my fellow students in the doctoral program at Duke University, and to my colleagues in the Departments of Religion of Campbell College and Florida State University.

Finally, a sincere word of gratitude must be said to the gentleman whose work is the subject of this volume. Mr. Walter Lippmann was unfailingly gracious and cooperative. He was prompt in correspondence, answered queries frankly and helpfully, and, by his interest, encouraged the progress of the study. For me to have moved among the landmarks of his intellectual and spiritual pilgrimage has been a rare and fruitful experience.

CHARLES WELLBORN

Florida State University
March, 1968

Contents

TWENTIETH CENTURY
PILGRIMAGE

Political ideas acquire operative force in human affairs when . . . they acquire legitimacy, when they have the title of being right which binds men's consciences. Then they possess, as the Confucian doctrine has it, "the mandate of heaven."

WALTER LIPPMANN

Introduction

To speak of "the mandate of heaven" within the context of political criticism and theory strikes many modern men as dogmatically presumptuous and uncomfortably metaphysical. Used with studied intent by Walter Lippmann, whom one observer has called "the most important American political thinker of the twentieth century," the choice of words is especially surprising.[1] Considered in the light of a long tradition in political philosophy, however, the term is not unusual. At least since the days of Confucius and, in Western thought, Sophocles, men seeking to reason out the whys and wherefores of politics have made connections of one kind or another between earth and heaven.

Plato's "republic," Augustine's "two cities," the "holy commonwealth" of the Puritans, the "inalienable rights" of the American Founding Fathers—each illustrates the tendency to find in political structures meaning which reaches beyond the material world. Representing the most fully developed, though certainly not the latest, member of this diverse family of thought was

[1] *The Public Philosophy* (New York, 1955), 138. For the quoted reference to Lippmann, see Clinton Rossiter and James Lare (eds.), *The Essential Lippmann* (New York, 1963), xi.

Thomas Aquinas, with his great synthesis of the natural and the supernatural. Indeed, what is called the "medieval spirit" consisted essentially of "a system of thoughts which culminated in the idea of a community which God himself had constituted and which comprised all Mankind." [2] As a shadow of the eternal, the political structure of that community ideally outlined the government of God.

Though a considerable segment of contemporary political science no longer regards this approach as productive, not everyone has abandoned it. Indeed, it will be argued here that this dimension of meaning—the attempt to link earthly political structures with some ultimate pattern of reality—undergirds Walter Lippmann's understanding of his own task as a political philosopher. He does not conceive of himself as simply theorizing in terms of intellectual abstractions, related neither to the concrete but transient realities of political life nor to the spiritual and eternal values of undistorted truth. Rather, political reality for him is a matter of two realms—that of existence, the common human condition, and that of essence, the world beyond or underlying existence, in which men's souls can be regenerate and at peace.[3] For Lippmann, political philosophy arises out of the inevitable tension between the two realms.

When a thinker operates with such presuppositions, his thought is open to fruitful analysis. A study of Lippmann's political theory, for instance, promises to reveal his concept of the nature of the world in which men carry out political actions, as well as his view of the nature of man himself. Such understandings are silhouetted against the background of what Lippmann conceives to be men's proper relationship to the structure of reality.

In recent years Professor Eric Voegelin has built a complex and persuasive philosophy of history on the assertion that a political society tends to express itself in symbols which are indicative of its self-understanding as representative of transcendent truth and

[2] Otto Gierke, *Political Theories of the Middle Ages*, trans. F. W. Maitland (Cambridge, 1900), 4.
[3] *The Public Philosophy*, 110.

reality. "Man does not wait for science to have his life explained to him, and when the theorist approaches social reality, he finds the field preempted by what may be called the self-interpretation of society." [4] To state it more simply, a community articulates itself in terms of structures of order which have underlying spiritual meaning. Accordingly, political philosophy can never begin with anything akin to John Locke's *tabula rasa*. Rather it works with a rich body of symbols and concepts provided by society and human experience, symbols which present themselves for critical clarification.

It follows that the work of a particular political theorist involves a continuous interaction between the concrete symbols of political order and his own personal theorizing. He cannot divorce himself from the structures about him, but his own theories, with roots in his existential understanding of self and society, may lead him to contradict those structures. Such clashes then become intellectual arenas for the continuing struggle to uncover meaning.

To accept the validity of this approach is to regard political theory as a discipline which has potential for the discernment of man's spiritual self-understanding. Accordingly, it is not surprising that terminology normally classified as religious shows up so frequently in this type of political theory. What such terms mean in any specific usage is a matter for definition, but one implication of their occurrence is certainly that political philosophy and religious theory, or theology, find some common ground and points of contact. That such a relation does, in fact, exist and that this relationship is both meaningful and fruitful for critical examination are two basic assumptions of this study of Walter Lippmann.

Why Lippmann? Primarily because as an intelligent, sensitive human being he has participated as both observer and actor in the intellectual and political life of the United States for more than fifty years, a major portion of the twentieth century. Although his first major book was published in 1913, he remains active and productive in the later years of the 1960's.[5] Note that

[4] Eric Voegelin, *Israel and Revelation* (Baton Rouge, 1957), ix.
[5] *A Preface to Politics* (New York, 1913).

the contention is not that Lippmann is, in any significant sense, a *typical* or *representative* twentieth century American. Does such a specimen actually exist? How would one identify him? Far from being average, Lippmann is intellectually head and shoulders above the mass of men; in addition, his career has afforded him access to areas of political experience that no ordinary men would be likely to encounter. Neither can Lippmann be considered simply a passive reflector of culture and society, since he has helped to mold and shape the thinking of a nation. In no way, however, do these facts disqualify him for the purposes of this study; instead, they add to his characterization as a remarkably sensitive antenna to the thought currents of the era.

Lippmann has not only lived the age, he has made his mark upon it, and in a strikingly coherent way he has been able to articulate the times. Indeed, he has consciously encountered, accepted, been influenced by, reacted against, or aided in formulating virtually every major movement in American philosophy and politics in this century. For this reason, his life and thought provide a window which permits us to see—not, to be sure, the whole interior of twentieth century man, but a fascinating and well-lighted room within that structure.

In these pages the development of Lippmann's thought across half a century is viewed as something of a pilgrimage, unfinished but always purposive, and therefore possessed of a degree of basic consistency. This contradicts many generally held estimates of Lippmann. As early as 1933, Amos Pinchot used the pages of *The Nation* to charge, "Not the least of the benefits of reading Mr. Lippmann is that he can be quoted on either side of almost any question." [6] The substance of the observation has since been repeated by others.

That there is superficial ground for this accusation cannot be denied. In the course of assessing day by day the rapidly changing political complexion of the nation, Lippmann has often altered his opinions concerning specific issues. His personal attitude in

[6] Amos Pinchot, "Walter Lippmann: I. The Great Elucidator," *Nation*, CXXXVII (July 5, 1933), 7

this regard may be gathered from some words he wrote in 1916 in defense of President Woodrow Wilson: "I see no virtue in the picture of the strong, obstinate, consistent man who never learns and never forgets."[7] Lippmann has often been willing to sacrifice iron-bound consistency for the open mind, ready to learn new lessons and correct old opinions. Consequently, it is not difficult to search his prolific writings of fifty years and emerge with a list of seeming contradictions.

Stubborn refusal to part with doctrinaire views is not the kind of consistency which is here attributed to Lippmann. When his life and thought are viewed as a pilgrimage, they are seen as maintaining a constant, fundamental integrity of goal and purpose. Lippmann has operated from a core of basic presuppositions— most of which have never been completely changed nor abandoned, though they have been gradually refined and modified. Throughout all of his professional life, Lippmann has addressed himself to the same essential political problem. His concern has been, above all else, for the effective functioning under modern conditions of the liberal democratic system of government in such a way as to preserve the most valuable possession of each individual human being—the integrity of his own personhood. This concern has led Lippmann down various paths of possible solution, many of which eventually had to be retraced or abandoned. He has analyzed democracy's maladies in different ways and varied his proposed antidotes according to his diagnosis. But the mature conclusions to which he has come, and in which he seems to rest at the present time, are fundamentally consistent with his life-long development.

In unique fashion Walter Lippmann has combined detailed attention to the dominant political events of his time with a constant quest for an overall frame of reference into which to fit the meaning of these events. Behind all of his astute commentary on current affairs lies a concern for the philosophical justification of the democratic state and society—a justification which involves,

[7] Lippmann, "The Case for Wilson," *New Republic*, VIII (October 14, 1916), 263.

for Lippmann, an extensive critique of the actual functioning of American democracy. His search for answers to what he considers the critical challenges to modern democracy has led him into philosophical and at least semi-theological investigations.

The heart of this study, therefore, is an attempt to explore the shape of this frame of reference in which Lippmann is able to find meaning for political events. To accomplish this requires a thorough examination of the changing patterns in Lippmann's thought across the years, especially in relation to four specific areas: the nature of man, the malady of democracy, the meaning and function of law, and the relevance of religion. In addition, the thought of Walter Lippmann is so inextricably intertwined with his life and experiences that it is impossible to understand its development apart from adequate biographical information. The biographical sketch which follows provides an opportunity to seek out the most significant influences—political, religious, and philosophical—which seem to have entered into the making of his mind.

Obviously, the American brand of democracy is now undergoing some of the most serious testings in its history. Strained both by external pressures of a costly, inconclusive, and unpopular war and the internal tension of threatening racial and political anarchy, the fabric of society seems ready to rip disastrously. As a result, the once-shining American vision is badly tarnished. To some, the "last best hope of mankind" appears destined only to take its place among humanity's discarded disappointments. At this crucial juncture the Republic needs all the collective wisdom of its citizens. Perhaps it can profit once more, as it has so often in the past, by listening to the voice of Walter Lippmann.

Damn it, I'm not going to spend my life writing bugle calls

WALTER LIPPMANN

Chapter I

A Biographical Sketch

Reminiscing in 1931 about the days of Walter Lippmann's tenure as editor of the New York *World,* novelist James M. Cain recalled a luncheon conversation:

"Well," I said, "if you ask me, the most that any newspaper should try to do is choose sides in a fight, and then fight as hard as it can, even when it secretly wishes the fight were going a little differently. But you are always trying to dredge up basic principles. In a newspaper, it won't work. For example, turn to music . . . a bugle has only four notes. Now if what you've got to blow is a bugle, there isn't any sense in camping yourself in front of piano music."

"You may be right," Lippmann said. "But damn it, I'm not going to spend my life writing bugle calls." [1]

In the ensuing years Lippmann has proved himself a versatile performer, rarely blowing the bugle, to be sure, but playing with ease and skill a variety of other instruments. He can be classified as a successful journalist, a practical political scientist, a political philosopher, a moral philosopher, a political economist, and an expert on foreign policy and international affairs. He has edited a

[1] James M. Cain, "The End of the *World,*" *The New Freeman,* II (1931), 612.

9

metropolitan newspaper, produced a popular column, written scholarly books, edited a book of poetry, composed sparkling personality sketches, and delivered university lectures. His multi-layered career has carried him from the cloisters of Harvard to the city hall of Schenectady; from Greenwich Village parties to the Paris Peace Conference; and from friendships with John Reed, the American Marxist, and Mabel Dodge Luhan, the "liberated" New York socialite, to associations with Woodrow Wilson, John Kennedy, Winston Churchill, and Nikita Khrushchev. Through it all he has sounded few bugle calls, insisting instead on trying to "dredge up basic principles."

Years ago, reviewing one of John Dewey's books, Lippmann commented that philosophy should always be seen as autobiography. Certainly, the developing patterns of his own thought reflect the multiplicity of influences that have come to bear upon him, along with the maturing experiences which have entered into the making of his mind and personality. Unfortunately, no entirely satisfactory biography of Lippmann has yet been written.[2] The sketch which follows attempts only to highlight the most significant events in a long and brilliant career.

City Sidewalks and Harvard Yard, 1889–1910

Walter Lippmann's roots go deep into the complex urban life of New York City. His father, Jacob Lippmann, a native New Yorker and a descendant of German-Jewish immigrants, was a well-to-do clothing manufacturer and real estate broker. His mother, Daisy Baum Lippmann, also a New Yorker and German-Jewish, was

[2] But see David E. Weingast, *Walter Lippmann* (New Brunswick, N.J., 1949), a fully documented volume which concentrates attention on an analysis of Lippmann's newspaper columns, particularly those from 1931 to 1940. Portions of Charles B. Forcey, *The Crossroads of Liberalism* (New York, 1961), which deal with Lippmann's early career, are valuable. Facts not otherwise documented in this chapter are largely drawn from these two sources. Also useful are John Mason Brown, *Through These Men* (New York, 1954), in which the section on Lippmann is based on personal interviews, and Marquis Childs and James Reston (eds.), *Walter Lippmann and His Times* (New York, 1959).

a Hunter College graduate who maintained a comfortable, secure, and cultured home.

An only child, Lippmann was born on September 23, 1889. At the age of seven, he entered Dr. Julius Sachs's School for Boys, an institution attended mostly by the sons of prosperous German-Jewish families. His educational and cultural development was not left, however, solely to his formal schooling. Travel to Europe was a regular part of his boyhood years, and once his parents took him as far as St. Petersburg and Moscow. Exposed to the best in painting, sculpture, music, architecture, and literature, he early acquired a familiarity with all the arts. Money was no problem, and the family emphasis was on what John Mason Brown has called "the civilized, the somewhat cottoned and cushioned, approach to life." [3]

Some religious training also entered into his experience. With his parents Lippmann attended Temple Emanu-El, located then at Fifth Avenue and Forty-third Street, where he received the conventional religious instruction offered by a Reform Jewish congregation. Despite this early formal connection, there is little evidence of deep impressions made on Lippmann by the Jewish faith.[4] He soon withdrew from any affiliation with a synagogue, and neither his first nor his second wife is Jewish.

Matriculating at Harvard University in 1906, Lippmann entered upon one of the decisive periods in his development. Seventeen years of age, aspiring to be an art critic, he found himself at Cambridge during the university's "golden age." President Charles W. Eliot had assembled a distinguished faculty; among its members

[3] Brown, *Through These Men*, 206.
[4] This is not to say that Lippmann can be understood apart from his Jewish background. At least one Jewish writer has sharply reproached Lippmann for not drawing more explicitly on his Hebrew heritage in the formation of his philosophic views: "Since Mr. Lippmann's deepest interest is, after all, in the good life, with morality, he might have saved some of that concern he lavishes on the decline of the supernatural Christianity of the Middle Ages for the fate of a tradition that more nearly shaped his own moral interest, namely, Judaism. Unluckily, Judaism does not exist for Mr. Lippmann. . . ." See Felix Morrow, "Religion and the Good Life," *The Menorah Journal*, XVIII (February, 1930), 103.

were William James, Josiah Royce, William Allen Neilson, Hugo Munsterberg, George Barrett Wendell, George Pierce Baker, and Albert Bushnell Hart. Eliot's educational philosophy represented nineteenth-century individualism at its height. His policy concerning students was "to allow each man to think and do as he pleases." [5] The students lived and ate where they chose, while the principal academic requirements were the freshman course in English, a reading knowledge of French and German, and attendance at lectures. Historian Samuel Eliot Morison, who was at Harvard at the same time as Lippmann, has said of the university: "A lad who came to Harvard with the makings of a genius did not have his little spark quenched or ambition trammeled upon; conversely, the boy who entered as a fool was very apt to graduate as a damned fool." [6]

Walter Lippmann was no fool—not when he entered Harvard and certainly not when he left. He found the college emphasis upon freedom and autonomy thoroughly congenial. Having completed the requirements for his bachelor's degree in three years, acquiring a Phi Beta Kappa key in the process, he decided to remain a fourth year as a graduate assistant in philosophy to Professor George Santayana.

Much of Lippmann's Harvard recognition came slowly. One of his classmates has described him as "suddenly emerging from three years of silence." [7] But when distinction did come, it arrived in impressive form. A book review Lippmann had written for the *Harvard Monthly* attracted the attention of William James, who then visited the student in his room. As a result of this initial contact, Lippmann, who had no classes under James, came under his personal influence and often joined other students in discussions at the philosopher's home. Santayana also took notice of Lippmann and counted him, along with T. S. Eliot, among his brightest students.

[5] Granville Hicks, *John Reed* (New York, 1936), 26. For an interesting description of life at Harvard in this period, see pp. 24–50.

[6] Samuel Eliot Morison, *Three Centuries at Harvard, 1636–1936* (Cambridge, Mass., 1936), 428.

[7] Hicks, *John Reed*, 48.

Recognition came, too, from his fellows. John Reed, the volatile future revolutionary who was to write *Ten Days That Shook the World*, once grandly introduced Lippmann at an eating club with the words, "Gentlemen, the future President of the United States." [8] And it was also Reed who poetically summed up, half-seriously and half-satirically, the impression Lippmann made on his associates:

> LIPPMANN,—calm, inscrutable,
> Thinking and writing clearly, soundly, well;
> All snarls of falseness swiftly piercing through,
> His keen mind leaps like lightning to the True;
> His face is almost placid,—but his eye,—
> There is a vision born to prophecy!
> He sits in silence, as one who has said:
> "I waste not living words among the dead!"
> Our all-unchallenged Chief! . . .[9]

What were the principal influences on Lippmann's thought during the Harvard years? Certainly, his academic work laid an intellectual foundation for the future, and a listing of his college courses gives some indication of the direction of his interests. Of the twenty-three full or half-year courses comprising his college program, seven were in philosophy; six in French, Latin, and Italian; five in economics, government, and history; three in English and comparative literature; and the remaining two in fine arts and social ethics.

Foremost among the dominant influences of these years were two teachers, James and Santayana. James was near the end of his career (he died in 1910, the year Lippmann left Harvard). Santayana was in his forties. Frequent quotes from and references to both men mark many of Lippmann's writings; and in an appendix to *A Preface to Morals*, he specifically designated the two, along with the English sociologist, Graham Wallas, as preeminent shapers of his own development.[10] James and Santayana made a strange combination. They respected each other but rarely agreed. James referred to

[8] *Ibid.*, 34.
[9] John Reed, *The Day in Bohemia* (New York, 1913), 42.
[10] *A Preface to Morals* (New York, 1929), 331.

Santayana's doctoral thesis as "the perfection of rottenness," [11] and Santayana, in turn, described portions of James's thought as "romantic cosmology." [12] Between the two a temperamental opposition ran deep. Yet Lippmann absorbed from both of them, and they left imprints upon his thinking which have been manifest throughout his career.

Shortly after he left Harvard, Lippmann wrote a brief tribute to James. Clearly set out are those aspects of the philosopher's thought which had impressed him most vividly. As might be expected, he admired James's open mind, which he interpreted as characteristic of a democratic outlook. James's willingness to give all men, all ideas, all creeds a hearing was the essence of democracy in action. Such an attitude also demonstrated an admirable humility of spirit. "James knew that he didn't know. He never acted upon the notion that the truth was his store of wisdom." [13]

Perhaps even more meaningful for young Lippmann, however, were the practical calls for concrete decision issuing from the philosophy of James. Full of enthusiasm, chafing for a taste of significant events, Lippmann was eager to find justification for moving ahead vigorously, both in his personal life and with the challenge of solving society's problems. In his article he recalled some of James's words: "The scientific demand that men should wait till doomsday, or till such time as our senses and intellect working together may have raked in evidence enough . . . is, says James, 'the queerest idol ever manufactured in the philosopher's cave.' " Life does not stand still; choices cannot be avoided. Absolute certainty is not humanly possible; therefore, men must find ways to act without it.

[11] Cited in Bertrand Russell, A History of Western Philosophy (New York, 1945), 811. Santayana has asserted that what James objected to was "my aestheticism, that seemed to find the highest satisfaction in essence or ideals, apart from their eventual realization in matters of fact." See Santayana, "Apologia Pro Mente Sua," in Paul Arthur Schilpp (ed.), The Philosophy of George Santayana (Evanston, Ill., 1940), 499.

[12] Cited in A Preface to Politics, 233.

[13] Lippmann, "An Open Mind: William James," Everybody's Magazine, XXIII (1910), 800–801. Quotations in the next two paragraphs are also from this article.

What ought to be the determining factor in the making of these necessary choices? Lippmann understood James to say that no one should refuse men the right to act upon "what seems to be most adapted to our needs." James argued that the final measure of truth lies in the practical consequences which follow any action. *"The true . . . is only the expedient in our way of thinking, just as the right is only the expedient in our way of behaving."* [14] If an hypothesis works, in that it enables one to deal with reality satisfactorily, it is true in the only sense of truth that actually matters.

An important aspect of James's influence was a strong strain of incipient anti-intellectualism. The pragmatic philosophy elevated the will above reason, demanding choice prior to the possession of completely logical grounds. James advised his followers to give up logic "fairly, squarely, and irrevocably," and to substitute "reality, life, experience, concreteness, and immediacy." Men must be ready "to live today by what truth we can get, and be ready tomorrow to call it falsehood." [15] Thus, his "radical empiricism" was well-fitted to open the door to philosophies with even stronger irrational elements, such as those of Henri Bergson and Georges Sorel, upon both of whom Lippmann relied heavily in the writing of A *Preface to Politics*.[16]

Lippmann enthusiastically embraced the bulk of James's teaching, and his first two books on politics were attempts to apply what he understood to be James's pragmatic principle.[17] Still, he must have had some doubts, for he never admitted to being a full-fledged pragmatist. Even in A *Preface to Politics*, his first important book, he pointed out certain deficiencies in James's thought.[18] In later years Lippmann recalled that it was Santayana who kept him from becoming a total pragmatist. The Spanish-

[14] William James, *The Meaning of Truth* (New York, 1909), viii. The italics are in the original.

[15] William James, *Pragmatism* (New York, 1928), 223.

[16] See esp. pp. 111, 170, 208, 227–32, 313.

[17] Cf. A *Preface to Politics*, 225, 236; and *Drift and Mastery* (New York, 1914), 261–63, 295.

[18] Cf. A *Preface to Politics*, 113–14.

born philosopher rejected James's concept of reality and posited a realm of "essences," immanent in the totality of nature, never wholly accessible, but approachable only through the life of intelligence and reason.[19] Existence is not subjective; the natural world is a world of objective reality. But "imagination and thought are immediate experiences as much as sensation is: they are therefore . . . no less actual ingredients of reality."[20] In opposition to James, Santayana exalted the use of man's rational powers as the prime determinant of choice. "The function of reason," he wrote, "is to dominate experience."[21]

For Santayana the achievement of the good life was the work of intelligent aestheticism; as such, it could be accomplished only by an aesthetic aristocracy. The good was the harmonious, and one achieved maturity only when he was in harmony with self, society, and the universe. Lippmann's own aesthetic background and interests made him sympathetic to this attitude—a point of view which played a major role in the development of his later moral thought, expressed in such books as A Preface to Morals. In the earlier years, however, his own outlook leaned much more in the direction of William James.

In addition to his contacts with James and Santayana, a third Harvard relationship helped materially to shape Lippmann's future. In the spring of 1910 the English Socialist Graham Wallas was a visiting professor, and Lippmann took his course. Since Lippmann was already a professed Socialist, it was not Wallas' Socialist ideas which were most influential. This "rather slovenly, slightly pedantic, noble-spirited" teacher (as H. G. Wells de-

[19] Santayana's concept of reason was much broader than the ordinary definition of the word. "The Life of Reason is accordingly neither a mere means nor a mere incident in human progress; it is the total and embodied progress itself, in which the pleasures of sense are included so far as they can be intelligently enjoyed and pursued. To recount man's rational moments would be to take an inventory of all his goods. . . ." See Santayana, "Reason in Common Sense," in The Life of Reason (New York, 1962), IV, 17.

[20] Santayana, Character and Opinion in the United States (New York, 1920), 80.

[21] Santayana, "Reason in Common Sense," 160.

scribed him),[22] was not simply an ivory-tower theorist. Wallas had been in the thick of London politics as a five-time candidate for office, and his ideas carried with them the weight of realism. His own experiences had left him somewhat disillusioned with political activism, as well as acutely aware of the inherent weaknesses of abstract political theory. As a result, he insisted that at the center of any valid political philosophy must stand the human individual, not just in terms of his theoretical needs and legal rights, but realistically conceived as a functioning person. He contended that abstractions, however logical and systematic, are fatal unless based on a consideration of human motivations. Men do not automatically think of ends and rationally calculate means, argued Wallas; they are guided partially by instinct and impulse. Successful politics must take these sub-rational motivations into account. Said Lippmann in *A Preface to Politics*: "I think we may say that his [Wallas'] is the distinction of having turned the study of politics back to the humane tradition of Plato and Machiavelli—of having made man the center of political investigation." [23]

Lippmann's openness to the human concern espoused by Wallas demonstrated itself in a strong awareness of social problems and injustice. Along with other students, he worked as a volunteer in such welfare institutions as Hale House and Civic Service House in downtown Boston, and in 1908 he spent several days of labor in the slums of Chelsea, where a major fire had left many families homeless and destitute. His articles in the Harvard student publications, written during this time, displayed concentrated interest in the welfare and rights of the economic and political underdogs of society.

In June, 1910, Lippmann's Harvard period came to an end. Abandoning his quest for a graduate degree, he decided to enter upon a career in journalism and politics. His ideas were in ferment; the pragmatism of James, the central human emphasis of

[22] Cited in Brown, *Through These Men*, 212.
[23] *A Preface to Politics*, 76–77. Wallas' ideas are most clearly developed in his *Human Nature in Politics* (New York, 1921).

Wallas, and the naturalistic intellectualism of Santayana mingled with the manifold other influences to which he had been exposed in his days of formal education. It would have been difficult for any observer accurately to predict the eventual direction in which Walter Lippmann, fresh from Harvard, might go.

"Mover and Shaker," 1910–25

The immediate course of Lippmann's experience, following his departure from Harvard, must be seen against the background of his socialist activities, which began while he was still a student. To young Lippmann, emerging from a home environment of comfort and culture into his first grating awareness of social unrest and human misery, socialism had made a powerful appeal. Full of youthful idealism, he was living in what he was to look back upon as "the soft air of the world before the wars." [24] Society's problems were complex, but solutions were available. Obvious injustices existed, but as a "brilliant young intellectual just out of Harvard," Lippmann "seems never to have doubted that the means to right these wrongs were ready and waiting." [25]

Social concern showed both in his articles written for the college publications and in his actions. In print, he argued for the teaching of Socialist doctrines in the classroom, championed the cause of woman's suffrage, and defended Wallas' brand of socialism over against Marxism. In action, he prodded the Harvard Socialist Club, of which he became president in 1909, to be more than a discussion group. The club drew up a Socialist platform for city elections, criticized the university for not paying its employees living wages, and lobbied for social legislation in the Massachusetts legislature. For a young liberal, eager and energetic, these experiences provided a tantalizing taste of what he imagined active political life to be. By June of 1910, he was ready to leave Harvard for the arena of practical politics.

[24] *The Public Philosophy*, 12.
[25] Marquis Childs, "Introduction: The Conscience of the Critic," in Childs and Reston (eds.), *Walter Lippmann and His Times*, 3.

A temporary job as a reporter for the Boston *Common,* a re-formist newspaper, was Lippmann's bridge from school to his pro-fession. The job, which began on a part-time basis even before he left school, came about through the influence and recommenda-tion of two notable Lippmann friends. One was Ralph Albertson, a leading Boston liberal who was head of the executive committee which published the *Common.* Albertson was an ordained Christian minister and an advocate of Christian socialism. Lippmann spent much time in the Albertson home during his Harvard days, became an intimate family friend, and finally, in 1917, seven years after he graduated, married Faye Albertson, the oldest daughter.

Lippmann's other friend was the journalist and muckraker Lincoln Steffens, who had taken on the young reporter as a sort of protege. After a short stint on the *Common* staff, Lippmann was engaged as Steffens' secretary and assistant at *Everybody's Magazine,* where the writer was an associate editor.[26] His associa-tion with Steffens was valuable training although he developed no great enthusiasm for muckraking. His published work during this period consists largely of commonplace pieces about such matters as pension frauds and arson. One article, however, stands out. Under the provocative title "The Most Dangerous Man in the World" it dealt with the French thinker Henri Bergson. In words which conveyed the optimistic tenor of his own outlook, Lipp-mann called Bergson "a fountain of energy, brilliant, terrifying, and important." His emphasis on the ceaseless flux of existence excited Lippmann most—his rejection of "a world once and for all fixed." The forms of life and society were not sacred. Men could and should employ their vibrant inner energies to change and revolutionize these forms. "It is the conservatives who violate the spirit of life when they want institutions to stay frozen tight, not the radicals who want them fluid." From this perspective Lippmann considered Bergson dangerous: "If I were interested

[26] Steffens had wagered his editor that he could create within six months an accomplished magazine writer from some intelligent college graduate. Lippmann was his "guinea pig." See Lincoln Steffens, *Autobiography* (New York, 1931), 592–93.

in keeping churches, consitutions, and customs fixed so that they would not change, I should regard Bergson as the most dangerous man in the world." [27]

At *Everybody's Magazine*, the young journalist's progress was spectacular. From his position as Steffens' assistant he was quickly promoted to an editorship of his own, but he found the work routine and confining.[28] When, in January, 1912, he was offered a position as assistant to the newly-elected Socialist mayor of Schenectady, New York, the Reverend George H. Lunn, he quickly accepted. In Schenectady, for the first time, Lippmann had opportunity to see some of his theoretical convictions under fire in a practical political situation. He was a part of the governing machinery of the largest city in the United States, with the exception of Milwaukee, under Socialist control. But how much of a Socialist was Lippmann?

Clearly, he was not a Marxist and never had been. Even before his contact with Graham Wallas, and certainly thereafter, he was committed to the gradual achievement of social reforms through parliamentary political action, rather than through revolution. His actual activity in the Socialist Party after he left Harvard is a matter of some dispute. According to one writer, Lippmann held membership for a time in the "most radical of the socialist groups in New York City." [29] Another maintains that he was secretary to the party's "cabinet" in New York State.[30] Certainly, if Lippmann ever was a dedicated and radical Socialist, this was the logical time. In New York City and Greenwich Village he was associated with a remarkable group of rebels, reformers, and revolutionaries. Looking back in 1930, Lippmann reminisced that "we had, I think, vague notions that mankind, liberated from want and drudgery,

[27] Lippmann, "The Most Dangerous Man in the World," *Everybody's Magazine,* XXVII (1912), 100–101.

[28] Lippmann found himself, as he remembers, occupied as the "first-reader of manuscripts and the sorter-out of jokes for a funny column." See Forcey, *The Crossroads of Liberalism,* 104.

[29] Ernest Sutherland Bates, "Walter Lippmann: The Career of Comrade Fool," *Modern Monthly,* VII (June, 1933), 269.

[30] Forcey, *The Crossroads of Liberalism,* 102.

would spend its energies writing poetry, painting pictures, exploring the stellar spaces, singing folk songs, dancing with Isadora Duncan in public squares, and producing Ibsen in little theaters." [31] His close friendship with John Reed and Mabel Dodge Luhan brought him into contact with such people as Bill Haywood, the one-eyed Marxist labor leader who eventually died in Russia; Max Eastman; Isadora Duncan; and Margaret Sanger.[32] With Reed and others, he helped produce a Madison Square Garden pageant dramatizing the demands of I.W.W. (Industrial Workers of the World) strikers in the Paterson, New Jersey, silk mills.

Whatever Lippmann's feelings were when he went to Schenectady, his four months as a city official were disillusioning ones. He quickly came to feel that Mayor Lunn was attempting to execute a program for which the people were neither politically nor intellectually prepared.[33] Moreover, he concluded that many of the Socialist politicians themselves did not adequately comprehend their own program. Consequently, the gap between the theoretical and the practical was almost insuperable. In *A Preface to Politics* (1913) Lippmann gave a highly critical, though tolerant, evaluation of socialism in general. By 1914, when he wrote *Drift and Mastery*, he had become openly hostile to much of the socialist scheme. "In America," he concluded, "socialist thinking has almost come to a standstill." [34]

Putting Lippmann's early socialism in proper perspective helps give a more accurate picture of the course of his political and ideological changes. As early as 1922 and continuing into the thirties, it was fashionable for left-wingers to castigate Lippmann as a renegade and a turncoat, a "tired liberal." He had moved, they charged,

[31] Lippmann, "Free Time and Extra Money," *Woman's Home Companion,* LVII (April, 1930), 31

[32] The fact that Haywood had lost an eye in a labor battle provoked Mabel Dodge Luhan's oft-quoted comment on Lippmann: "Walter was never, never going to lose an eye in a fight. 'He might,' I thought, 'lose his glow, but he will never lose an eye.'" See Mabel Dodge Luhan, *Movers and Shakers* (New York, 1936), 119

[33] For an account of the Schenectady experience, see Lippmann, "Two Months in Schenectady," *The Masses,* III (April, 1912), 13.

[34] *Drift and Mastery,* 312.

all the way from Marxism to reactionary right-wing conservatism. The truth seems to be that he never seriously occupied either of these extreme positions. The matter of reactionary conservatism will be considered later, but the characterization of Lippmann as a Marxist is manifestly incorrect. It is not even clear that he was ever a "good" Socialist, at least doctrinally. His radicalism appears to have been a part of the youthful temper of his generation. As he wrote in 1909, "There is nothing ridiculous in being dissatisfied; it is decidedly ridiculous for young men to be 'conservative,' for it means that they will probably be 'stand-patters' when they grow older. Men who are 'orthodox' when they are young are in danger of being middle-aged all their lives." [35] From the beginning Lippmann was sensitive to the maladjustments and inadequacies of existing democratic society. He was concerned with improvement and worthwhile change. To him, as to most of his college friends, socialism came close to meaning humanitarianism. It was "socialism of the heart" and "social gospelism." [36]

Lippmann's experience in the Schenectady mayor's office modified his convictions about his own role in politics. He concluded that he was not cut out to be an office holder, administering policy, but that his job was to attempt to clarify issues and to promote "the revolution in men's minds" which he had come to believe must precede any significant social action. He had begun to doubt the practical wisdom of radical dependence on the democratic principle of majority rule. The majority in Schenectady so often seemed to have no understanding of what was involved in their decisions. "To me," he wrote, "it always seemed that we were like Peer Gynt struggling with the unwatered hinterland of the citizens of Schenectady." [37]

Leaving Schenectady, Lippmann wanted to put on paper some of his reflections and thus begin his work of political education. The result was A Preface to Politics, written largely during the

[35] Lippmann, "Harvard in Politics: A Problem in Imperceptibles," *Harvard Monthly, XLIX* (December, 1909), 98.
[36] Weingast, *Walter Lippmann,* 11.
[37] *A Preface to Politics,* 183.

summer of 1912 in a cabin in the Maine woods. The book is a remarkable accomplishment for a young man of twenty-three, just two years out of college. Lippmann, looking back on it, has commented humorously that it covered "pretty nearly all human problems." Nevertheless, it was well-received both by critics and by the public. Ex-President Theodore Roosevelt was enthusiastic about it, and the Boston *Transcript* called it "in many respects . . . the ablest brief book of its kind, published during the last ten years." [38]

Essentially, the *Preface* represented an attempt to apply a combination of Graham Wallas' insights into human nature and William James's pragmatism to the practical problems of politics. There were frequent references to Bergson, H. G. Wells, and Georges Sorel, the French syndicalist. Perhaps the most striking feature of the book, however, was its heavy debt to the psychological discoveries and theories of Sigmund Freud. The Freudian references reflected an interesting background.

With Lippmann in Maine during the summer he wrote his book was a close friend, Alfred Kuttner, who was engaged in translating Freud's recent *An Interpretation of Dreams*. Lippmann read the translation as it progressed and later wrote, "I . . . began to see how much Freud had to contribute to the psychology I had learned in college." [39] To someone who had rejected most traditional objective sources of authority as unworthy of confidence, Freud's introspective, non-evaluative approach to the irrational depths of the human personality made a strong appeal. To Lippmann, Freud's ideas appeared to supply the new psychology of human nature for which Graham Wallas had called. Freud argued that the two fundamental human drives are hunger and sex, the ego instinct and the erotic instinct. Civilized living, including politics, necessitates the sublimation or redirection of these urges. The presence of good and evil in the world is not evidence of conflicting moral and immoral drives and desires in the human personality. The difference arises solely out of the differing nature of the modes of

[38] Cited in Forcey, *The Crossroads of Liberalism*, 110.
[39] *Ibid.*, 109.

expression. On this basis, Lippmann argued, "much the same energies produce crime and civilization, art, vice, insanity, love, lust, and
religion." [40] The aim of politics is not to judge these desires but to
fit itself to them so as to aid in redirecting them into acceptable
channels. Man's natural instincts are the key to political understanding; to meet and satisfy them in a constructive manner is the
aim of political action. That this application of Freudian theory to
politics constituted an acceptable interpretation of the implications
of psychoanalysis was substantiated by a highly favorable review of
A *Preface to Politics*, which appeared in Freud's own magazine.[41]

While Lippmann had been busy in the Maine woods with his
manuscript, the presidential campaign of 1912 was in full swing.
His literary preoccupation prevented his taking any active part in
the election preliminaries, but the pages of A *Preface to Politics* reveal his admiration for Theodore Roosevelt, the Progressive or "Bull
Moose" candidate. Lippmann had little respect for President Taft,
the Republican choice for reelection, disdainfully dubbing him
"the perfect routineer." Woodrow Wilson, the Democratic Party
nominee, he admired for his intellect, "the clean and athletic quality of his thinking," but Wilson had degraded himself by accepting
"a futile and intellectually dishonest platform." [42]

Lippmann cannot be said to have been blind to Roosevelt's
faults and weaknesses. He characterized him as crude whereas Wilson was subtle, but his overall judgment was that Roosevelt, more
than any other figure on the political scene, was "the working
model for a possible American statesman at the beginning of the
Twentieth Century." Back in New York City with his completed
book, the young author heard Colonel Roosevelt in his final campaign address in Madison Square Garden. The candidate had been
shot by a fanatic in Milwaukee and, as a result, had missed much
of the campaign while recuperating. The rally must have been a
dramatic and moving occasion. Twenty-three years afterward,

[40] A *Preface to Politics*, 51.
[41] See Ernest Jones, review of Lippmann's A *Preface to Politics*, in *Imago*
(Vienna), II (1913), 452–56.
[42] A *Preface to Politics*, 55.

Lippmann recalled "that great night . . . when Roosevelt spoke after he had been shot . . . I was his unqualified hero worshipper." [43] Looking back, Lippmann classed himself as among those who, using Roosevelt's own charismatic phrase, "stood at Armageddon and battled for the Lord."

Lippmann's attachment for Theodore Roosevelt and the "New Nationalism" was not surprising. The times demanded "innovators" with verve and enthusiasm. In the Bull Moose candidate, Lippmann saw a strong and imaginative leader with a sure sense for those human needs, drives, and passions emphasized in the *Preface*. His Progressive policies—the graduated income tax, the substitution of a positive and healthy governmental regulation of big business for the negative and ineffective Sherman Anti-Trust Act, a powerful national government, lower tariffs, and increased social welfare legislation—all appealed to Lippmann, fresh from his Socialist misadventure and seeking a forward-looking but more attainable political program. It is not clear whether he ever actually thought Roosevelt could be elected; but, win or lose, he felt the Progressive Party would become a badly-needed, fresh, new force in American politics. What Lippmann, along with many other Progressives, did not realize was how completely the Progressive Party was constructed around the personality of Roosevelt. When the election was lost, the candidate, to the consternation of his followers, began a gradual return to the Republican Party. Soon Lippmann had to search for a new political hero.

Lippmann's second published attempt at political analysis, *Drift and Mastery*, was written less than a year after *A Preface to Politics*; yet remarkable changes of thought and perspective were evident in its pages. Most significant was Lippmann's unmistakable retreat from his earlier flirtations with irrationalism. In the brief period of one year he had become markedly more enthusiastic about the ability of science to offer answers to society's problems. In words that obviously applied to Bergson, whom he had quoted with approval in his earlier book, he characterized "that sense of

[43] *A Tribute to Theodore Roosevelt*, October 27, 1858–1935 (n.p., 1935), 1.

'vital urge' which is so common today" as being an "emotion of futurity" which would "fritter itself away unless it comes under the scientific discipline." Despite this pronouncement and his statement that "we have a right to call science the discipline of democracy," Lippmann did not move all the way into the camp of scientism. He was still suspicious of pure reason, and he continued to insist that any approach to human problems must take into consideration the full span of human motivations, both reasonable and emotional. Science, he argued, must become "its own critic . . . forestall its own timidities, and control its own bias." His basic rule was still a pragmatic one; he quoted William James: "Use concepts when they help, and drop them when they hinder understanding." [44]

Though Bergson was criticized, Sorel ignored, and Freud barely mentioned, James and Wallas remained as guiding spirits in this book, even as in the earlier one. Now, however, the pragmatic attitude, coupled with a new awareness of certain aspects of human nature, produced for Lippmann new insights. He thought American business, for instance, had undergone a reorganization so radical that few had perceived its significance. The control of business was passing from the old-fashioned profiteer to a new class—the managers. Complex business operations required the supervision of an expert, just as the practical approach to other forms of social organization demanded the efforts of the scientist. Lippmann's perception of the revolutionary change in business structure involved in the rise of the managerial class was a thesis that did not receive general recognition until twenty years later.[45] His optimistic hopes reflected his high estimate—indeed, almost reverence—for the *expert*. The problems of the world were largely those of drift; they could be mastered by men who knew what they were doing and where they were going. Obviously, Lippmann's "experts" were not in charge of contemporary political affairs, for the nations moved

[44] *Drift and Mastery,* 275, 155, 274, 160.
[45] Cf., e.g., Adolf A. Berle, Jr. and Gardiner C. Means, *The Modern Corporation and Private Property* (New York, 1937).

inexorably into global conflict. The challenge was to discover such men.

Shortly before completing *Drift and Mastery*, Lippmann became one of the editors of a fledgling magazine called the *New Republic*. The first edition appeared on November 7, 1914. At its beginning, the journal was strongly under the influence of Roosevelt's exuberant personality. All three of the principal editors, Herbert Croly, Walter Weyl, and Lippmann, had supported the Bull Moose effort, Croly and Weyl more actively than Lippmann. But Lippmann was by now equally under Roosevelt's spell, and during the planning stage of the magazine the three men had a number of personal contacts and conferences with the ex-President. This close association was not destined to last. In December, only a month after the *New Republic* began publication, Roosevelt wrote an article for the New York *Times* which vehemently attacked President Wilson's Mexican policy. "It seemed to us a brutally unfair attack," wrote Lippmann later, "and though we criticized Wilson's Mexican policy, we criticized Roosevelt sharply. He reproached us bitterly and never forgave us." [46] Lippmann and his coworkers thus discovered that, at least in matters involving his arch-rival Wilson, Roosevelt could brook no disagreement. In the months that followed, the magazine praised and blamed both Roosevelt and Wilson, but eventually all of the editors moved into the political camp of the new President.

In the first months of the *New Republic*'s life the preeminent political fact was the destructive European war drawing ever closer to American interests and to American shores. Lippmann has recorded that Graham Wallas warned him as early as 1910 that there was a real danger of major war, but the sociologist's pessimism made little impression. When hostilities actually broke out, Lippmann was on a leisurely European vacation. In Belgium during the last week of July, 1914, he bought a railroad ticket for a journey through Germany to Switzerland and recalled later "being

[46] Lippmann, "Notes for a Biography," *New Republic*, LXIII (1930), 251.

astounded and rather annoyed when I went to the railroad station and found that the German border was closed because Belgium had had an ultimatum." His own verdict was that he was "one young man who was not mentally prepared for the age he was destined to live in." [47]

Through his writings for the *New Republic* during the first three years of the war, it is possible to trace Lippmann's thinking. As the repercussions of the war on American life slowly mounted, he became more conscious of the dimensions of the world crisis. In December, 1915, he summed up his estimate of the country's reactions. Typically, he attacked President Wilson for not supplying more positive leadership; at the same time, he reflected some of his own uncertainties as to the direction in which that leadership should go. "We have lived for seventeen months as the spectator of events that have no parallel in our lives. At first we were stirred as never before. . . . But this feeling has spent itself on nothing. We have had nothing to exercise our emotions upon, and we are choked by feelings unexpressed and movements arrested in mid-air. . . . We Americans have been witnessing supreme drama, clenching our fists, talking, yet unable to fasten any reaction to realities." [48] What did Lippmann see as the answer to these frustrations? Though he admitted to resentment at the invasion of Belgium and the sinking of the *Lusitania*, he was not yet prepared to abandon neutrality in fact, though clearly he had already abandoned it in opinion and sentiment. He wished instead for some genius of a leader who would "give our neutrality a positive meaning."

As the conflict continued, a growing awareness of the deep correlation between American and British interests possessed Lippmann. In January, 1916, he discussed the poor state of American relations with Britain, ending with the emphatic declaration that the government's policy toward Great Britain "will be a crowning disaster unless that policy is determined by a vision of the Anglo-American future." [49] Yet, even his mild Anglophilia (a continuing

[47] *U.S. Foreign Policy: Shield of the Republic* (Boston, 1943), xi–xii.
[48] Lippmann, "Uneasy America," *New Republic*, V (1915), 195.
[49] Lippmann, "Washington Notes," *New Republic*, V (1916), 335.

feature of his thought up to the present) had not yet pushed him to the point of demanding that the U.S. enter the war. He was assured in his own mind that "there is no feeling in Washington that war impends." The determining policy factor was the nation's overwhelming desire for peace, and President Wilson seemed committed to the fulfillment of that desire.

Confronting the presidential election of 1916, Lippmann was pessimistic about both major parties. America's foreign policy, as he saw it, was totally inadequate. No real preparation had been made for the possibility of war. Wilson had been unable to draw the nation together in the close national cohesion which Lippmann favored. He still saw Theodore Roosevelt as the man who might accomplish such a task, but Roosevelt's party attachments were against him. Lippmann's only bit of optimism, a frail prophecy of his coming allegiance, was reserved for a recent speech by Wilson in which the President had proposed a League to Enforce Peace.

Wilson was renominated, and the Republicans chose Supreme Court Justice Charles Evans Hughes. As the campaign progressed, Lippmann was more and more repelled by Republican strategy. They had but one issue, he asserted, and but one principle—a desire to beat Wilson. Their candidate was capable and honest but sadly unqualified for the particular demands of the presidency in the perilous days ahead. With the choice now resting between Wilson and Hughes, Lippmann made up his mind. On October 14, 1916, he announced his decision in an article entitled "The Case for Wilson." He saw the President as "evolving under experience and remaking his philosophy in the light of it." Wilson was, if even temporarily, creating a national liberal party out of the "reactionary, parochial fragments of the Democracy."[50] The Socialist turned Progressive had now become a Democrat.

Lippmann's switch to Wilson was not arbitrary. It can be traced to a compound of factors: the increasing need for strong leadership in the face of the worsening conflict in Europe; disillusionment with Theodore Roosevelt; disgust with the Republicans;

[50] Lippmann, "The Case for Wilson," 263–64.

and steadily increasing respect for the strength and basic liberalism of President Wilson. On the other hand, Lippmann's support of Wilson was not naive. He was not unaware of Wilson's limitations. Seeking to be both a pragmatist and a realist, he was forced to the conclusion that Wilson was the best available leader for the country.

During the next two years the editors of the New Republic were closer to Wilson than they had ever been to Roosevelt. Indeed, the legend developed that the New Republic was Wilson's press outlet. Still, Lippmann asserted later, there was never a significant personal relationship with the President. He and Herbert Croly became friends of Colonel Edward M. House, Wilson's closest personal adviser, and they discussed political problems with him "perhaps once a fortnight." Presumably, House passed on some of their thinking to the President. But, maintained Lippmann, "we never knew any secrets, we never had a request to publish or not to publish anything, and we were not in a confidential relationship." [51]

In the early days of 1917 the New Republic strongly supported Wilson's attempts to achieve a "peace without victory" through a positive American policy of active pressure for negotiations among the European belligerents. But the attitude of the Central Powers, plus the resumption of unrestricted German submarine warfare, convinced the New Republic editors that there no longer existed any viable alternative for the United States other than a close and sympathetic alignment with the Allies. In its issue of February 7, 1917, the magazine called for a breaking-off of diplomatic relations with Germany and the initiation of conferences with the Allies relative to the terms and conditions of American entrance into the war. In little more than two months the U.S was at war.

Now Lippmann's life, like that of most other Americans, took a new turn. As in Schenectady, once more—and now for the last time—he played an active, immediate role in the shaping of government policy. Newton D. Baker, Wilson's Secretary of War, was a close friend, and he appointed Lippmann as an assistant, with the responsibility of handling labor relations in war production.

[51] Lippmann, "Notes for a Biography," 251.

Later, he was placed on a number of other government committees, on one of which Franklin D. Roosevelt, Assistant Secretary of Navy, also served. Lippmann's duties in Washington occupied him through the summer of 1917.

President Wilson was anxious to begin preparations for the coming peace negotiations. He organized a research body charged with accumulating relevant geographic, ethnic, and political data. Dr. Sidney E. Mezes, president of the College of the City of New York, was selected to head the group, and Lippmann was chosen as executive secretary. Using the simple title "The Inquiry," the organization functioned in secret.[52] In November, 1917, at the request of Wilson, it prepared a memorandum which was developed by the President into the substance of the famed Fourteen Points.

Despite the importance of his duties, Lippmann was restless. Accordingly, he accepted an assignment as an army captain to do political propaganda in France. With the impending collapse of German resistance, Lippmann was attached to Colonel House's staff in Paris. When the Germans offered to surrender on the basis of Wilson's Fourteen Points, British and Italian leaders asked for a clarifying explanation of the exact meaning of that document. Given the task of drafting the explanation, Lippmann did the job under pressure, working all night, and personally wrote memoranda on thirteen of the points. Frank Cobb, later to be Lippmann's superior on the New York *World*, wrote the fourteenth. After Wilson approved the draft, it was used as a basis for negotiations. Though Lippmann had serious doubts as to the wisdom of the President's personal participation in the Paris Peace Conference, he felt, nevertheless, that the acceptance by the Allies of the Fourteen Points as a basis for peace was a genuine victory. His optimism was destined for speedy shocks. It took only a little of the actual conference proceedings for Lippmann to understand what was happening to Wilson under the pressure of the other Allied leaders.

In February 1919, Lippmann left Paris to return to the United

[52] For an account of the work of "The Inquiry," see James T. Shotwell, *At the Paris Peace Conference* (New York, 1937), 3–19.

States and his job at the *New Republic*. His pessimistic outlook as to the outcome of the peace negotiations deepened, and by March the *New Republic* was editorially suggesting that even the friends of Wilson could only help save the proposed League of Nations by honest criticism of the Paris Conference. In late March the magazine called for the defeat of the controversial Article X of the Versailles Treaty, a provision which was designed to guarantee the territorial integrity of League members, but which Lippmann and others saw as a guarantee to the Allies of the spoils of victory. When the full text of the treaty was published, Lippmann's break with Wilson became complete. According to one account, he denounced the treaty "as a breaking of faith with Germany and a violation of moral obligations to the world." [53] Lippmann himself recalled, however, that the decision to oppose ratification was actually made by Croly, and "I followed him, though I was not then, and am not now, convinced that it was the wise thing to do. . . . If I had to do it all over again, I would take the other side; we supplied the Battalion of Death [the forces of isolation] with too much ammunition." [54]

Some years later, Lippmann could look back on Wilson with more objectivity than was possible in 1919. In 1927 he was able to judge that the President had sowed the seeds of "a triumph that may make him immortal." Yet, his picture of Wilson still reflected the profound intellectual shock that was Lippmann's principal legacy from his wartime experiences. In the war years Wilson had been, he said, a man doing against his will and judgment "what immeasurably great events were compelling him" to do. He had "to bow to a destiny that was overbearing him." [55] Such an understanding of Wilson's leadership was far different from that of Wilson as the intuitive master of history, riding the tide of great events, who had been Lippmann's ideal in his pre-war years.

For a brief time, Walter Lippmann had given himself, as did others, to the intoxicating promise of a crusade for world democ-

[53] Robert M. Lovett, *All Our Years* (New York, 1948), 172.
[54] Lippmann, "Notes for a Biography," 252.
[55] *Men of Destiny* (New York, 1927), 126–28.

racy and liberalism. He had tried his hand at blowing bugles, but the notes had seemed to go sour even as they were formed. It was time to return to the difficult task of dredging up principles, but the principles that were now to be set forth were inevitably colored by the stains of his disillusionment.

For Lippmann the period following the close of World War I was a time of adjustment and renewed analysis. The war had damaged his optimistic views about the ability of men, by the sheer power of careful thought and trained action, to stop society's drift and achieve mastery. His faith in the efficacy of strong, positive leadership had been shaken by the experiences of both Roosevelt and Wilson. Certainly, part of the fault lay in the personal defects of the two leaders. But was this the real answer? Lippmann was troubled by a nagging question: could *any leader*, however capable, facing those limitations under which the American President had to function, have done better? The tenets of the kind of nationalistic, optimistic liberalism which had undergirded the founding of the *New Republic* were now, for Lippmann, nebulous and uncertain, and his association with the magazine could not be entirely happy. In 1920 he resigned his position in order to write a book in which he hoped to deal with his new problems. After completing the manuscript of *Public Opinion*, published in 1922, he joined the staff of the liberal New York *World* as an editorial writer under Frank Cobb, with whom he had worked in Paris. In 1923, following Cobb's death, Lippmann succeeded him as editor.

In the first years of this period Lippmann became concerned with the nature of public consent in a democracy. He had argued earlier that the impulses and desires of the public, though often crude and in need of refinement, were generally to be trusted for the direction of basic political policy. The job of the statesman was to interpret these impulses and desires, both the rational and irrational ones, and to lead the people in the direction of positive and constructive fulfillment. Now Lippmann was disturbed by the fact that it was exactly this unrefined public opinion which appeared to have been the main villain in the drama of Wilson's failure. He had observed the consequences of what seemed to be Wilson's naive confidence in the character of popular support. Furthermore, during his war service he had studied the alarming potential of propaganda, and by the end of 1919 he had asserted that the "protection of the sources of opinion is the basic problem of democracy." [56] Discouraged by public misunderstanding and ignorance of what actually went on at the Paris Peace Conference, he was inclined to put primary blame on the newspapers who supplied their readers not with clearly interpreted facts but with twisted propaganda.

In a real sense, Lippmann felt, the post-war crisis of democracy was a "crisis in journalism." Democracy depended upon intelligent consent by the public; yet the manufacture of consent was an unregulated private enterprise. Society had become far too complex for any one man to understand it or to keep track of its operation. All men were at the mercy of the organs of information. By 1922 Lippmann had completed his major work on this special problem of democratic consent. *Public Opinion*, which is still regarded as a classic in its field, showed his painful rethinking of the type of liberalism which had characterized his earlier years. His attack now was aimed at the oversimplified concept that functioning democracy rested on the assumption of an informed, rational public. He argued that what man actually reacted to was not the substance of reality but "pictures in their heads," pictures which could be grotesquely distorted by modern media of communication. This volume will be discussed in more detail later, but what *Public Opinion* articulated clearly was Lippmann's growing distrust of the ability of the unaided masses to give rational consent or direction to the detailed affairs of a democracy. Only trained experts could perform this task.[57]

Against this background Lippmann obviously saw his own editorial work with the *World* and his subsequent syndicated column as part of a badly needed function of news clarification

[56] Lippmann, "The Basic Problem of Democracy," *Atlantic Monthly*, CXXIV (1919), 626.
[57] *Public Opinion* (New York, 1922), esp. 3–32, 379–97.

and interpretation. Later, during his first rush of national popularity with the New York *Herald-Tribune* an enthusiastic publicist dubbed him the "Great Elucidator." The title was not amiss, at least not in terms of his objective.

As editor of the *World* Lippmann found a wide audience for his talents. His editorials, restrained and scholarly, bore down heavily on the side of the public welfare as he saw it and against special privilege. The paper supported John Davis in the presidential election of 1924, and in 1928 was strongly committed to Alfred E. Smith, whose practical administrative abilities Lippmann especially admired. The *World* vigorously exposed the oil land scandals of the Harding era, battled the Ku Klux Klan, campaigned for better living and working conditions for West Virginia miners, and opposed the efforts of religious fundamentalists to prohibit the teaching of evolution in public schools.

Though these attitudes toward current issues were generally what might have been expected from his mildly radical background, an inner change was taking place in Lippmann. He had not forsaken the central human emphasis which was a part of his legacy from Graham Wallas. Neither was he ready to desert William James's insistence on the necessity of measuring practical consequences as a major determinant in choice. But the insights of his *New Republic* and World War I experiences were inescapable, and his studies of public consent had opened up disturbing vistas. Lippmann had to rethink his own attitudes. His resolution of the conflicts occasioned by this rethinking awaited explication in the publication of another landmark volume, *A Preface to Morals*.

Apostle of Disinterest, 1925–38

Lippmann had become convinced that the actual business of political administration and policy formulation could not be done by the masses; rather, these must be the work of a trained coterie of experts. In *The Phantom Public*, a sort of sequel to *Public Opinion*, he pushed the implications of his thought further and concluded that the effective area of public function was strictly limited to the role of determining whether the principals in public controversies were behaving according to accepted rules.[58] The public could not be expected to deal with the substance of political questions or produce a continuous directing force in public affairs. The role of the people was not to govern; instead, they should periodically mobilize and intervene in public affairs, choosing leadership by supporting those aspirants for power who were willing to adhere to fixed standards of political behavior.

Such a stance—a considerable modification of Lippmann's earlier counsel to trust the basic impulses of the masses—left him with knotty problems. Where does one obtain, for instance, the fixed standards to which public leaders must adhere? By what authority are they fixed? Perhaps even more basically, what kind of men must these leaders be, if they are adequately to discharge their tremendous responsibilities?

A *Preface to Morals* was Lippmann's first major try at an answer to these questions. As an attempt to delineate a nonmetaphysical, nonabsolutist ethic by which rational, civilized men could live in a complex, technological world, it was a broadly conceived project, touching many aspects of life. Politically, it aimed at defining such an ethic for those "mature men" whose responsibility was policy making and opinion formation.

The two *Prefaces* which Lippmann has written were separated in time by sixteen years; their philosophical separation was decisive. Left far back in the shadows by A *Preface to Morals* were Freud, Bergson, and Sorel, so influential in the earlier A *Preface to Politics*. Even much of the essential argument of James and Wallas had disappeared, though the importance of both was still acknowledged. What emerged instead was something akin to George Santayana's emphases on "essence," aestheticism, and the necessity for clear, harmonious reasoning. As the recommended "religion of the spirit"—in opposition both to supernaturalism and the harsh one-dimensional positivism of the scientist—Lippmann offered his own special brand of humanism. He conceived his audience to be that group of men in whom, to use the phrase

[58] *The Phantom Public* (New York, 1925).

he made famous, "the acids of modernity" had eaten away the ability to believe in a supernatural kingdom of God, yet who could not be satisfied with the ambiguity of "mere freedom." [59] Something positive had to replace the lost faith; a moral vacuum must be filled.

Lippmann's humanism, posed as a solution for this problem, had deep though apparently unacknowledged roots in the ancient teachings of the Stoics, particularly the thought of men like Marcus Aurelius.[60] Also present were strains of influence reaching back to Aristotle and Confucius. Added to the wisdom of these ancients was a dose of Jamesian pragmatism—an insistence that man's living faith must be correlated with the realm of human experience. For modern men the acceptance of intrinsic authority in some "higher law" or divine sanction was impossible; man's own nature, and that of the world in which he lives, must provide the guidelines. Humanism, Lippmann said, was characterized by "detachment, understanding, and disinterestedness in the presence of reality itself." [61] Implying a sort of intellectualization of one's emotions, "disinterestedness" was the key word. In much the same way as Marcus Aurelius had suggested, the individual must detach himself and his own desires from the rational consideration of such facts in experience as pain, evil, and death. Lippmann's humanist would deal analytically with these realities, thus rendering them emotionally harmless. Instead of being dominated by the irrationalities of life, he would relegate these irrationalities to their proper places in his experience. Though Lippmann recognized some similarity between his approach and Freud's psychoanalytical "catharsis of emotions," his estimate of the power of these drives and the ability of reason to master them took a different turn from that of the psychiatrist.

If society is to achieve its proper ends, mature men, practicing "disinterestedness," must direct its course. Lippmann's final descrip-

[59] A Preface to Morals, 8.

[60] Strangely, though the philosophical kinship is clear, no mention of or reference to either the Stoics or Marcus Aurelius appears in A Preface to Morals.

[61] A Preface to Morals, 221.

tion of one who belongs to this elite is strikingly stoic in character: "Since nothing gnawed at his vitals, neither doubt nor ambition, nor frustration, nor fear, he would move easily through life. And so whether he saw the thing as comedy, or high tragedy, or plain farce, he would affirm that it is what it is, and that the wise man can enjoy it." [62]

In the area of politics Lippmann's "high religion" of disinterestedness shaped a particular approach. Obeying the primary command of his old teacher Wallas, Lippmann sought to analyze the nature of man and then to draw his political precepts from that analysis. Man has the potential to become mature, he thought, in the sense of being morally disinterested. The business of government is to operate so as to make possible the kind of society in which this man can function most effectively. At the same time, the government must protect and refine the interests of the multitudes who have not achieved maturity.

The prime concern of government is, said Lippmann, not to manage the life of the community but to harmonize the direction which the community gives to its affairs. What the government should aim for is not to rule men but "to add overwhelming force to men when they rule their own affairs." In this conception of the role of the state—an approach which Lippmann derived directly from his understanding of the nature of man and the "good life" —lies the clue to a solution of the puzzle of his shift to anti-New Deal politics in the later thirties. In 1932, operating from his influential position as a widely-read columnist, he supported Franklin D. Roosevelt's bid for the Presidency against the incumbent, Herbert Hoover.[63] He recognized the depression of the early thirties as a major national crisis threatening the vitals of the country. Decisive, imaginative leadership was required, and he felt that Hoover was unable to provide it. Only massive governmental inter-

[62] *Ibid.*, 330.

[63] Lippmann's popularity was illustrated by the famed *New Yorker* cartoon which depicted two dowagers in a railroad dining car. One of them, looking at her newspaper, commented, "Of course, I only take a cup of coffee in the morning. A cup of coffee and Walter Lippmann is all I need."

vention could secure a stabilized economic system with adequate protection for the well-being of the people.

Lippmann, however, never conceived of the government's role as that of permanently directing a collectivized economy. "I do not regard the Roosevelt program as directed to the establishment of a planned economy," he wrote. He favored New Deal measures so long as they were conceived, on the one hand, as strictly emergency measures for a time of crisis, and on the other, as evidence of "an unwillingness to drift, and prudent, orderly thinking." [64] When, in his judgment, President Roosevelt's policies failed to measure up to these criteria, Lippmann did not hesitate to oppose him.

By the middle of 1935 Lippmann had grown increasingly skeptical of the New Deal's methods and objectives. He was unhappy with what he considered evidence of Roosevelt's lack of respect for the supremacy of law and the accountability of the government to the law—those "accepted standards of procedure" which had been central to the argument of *The Phantom Public*. His fears in this area led him to support the Republican nominee for President in 1936, Alfred M. Landon. It is fair to say that Lippmann displayed little or no real enthusiasm for Landon. He saw himself as choosing the lesser of two evils. The violent accusations by his critics that his basic views had drastically changed or that he had "sold out" to people of wealth and privilege show little understanding of the foundations behind his views.[65]

The politics of disinterestedness was given its fullest exposition in Lippmann's *The Good Society*, published in 1937. Here he somewhat indiscriminately lumped together various forms of what he considered to be collectivism, damning them all. The New Deal, Old Guard Republicanism, communism, and fascism were included

[64] Lippmann, "Today and Tomorrow" (New York *Herald-Tribune* syndicated daily newspaper column), February 1, April 20, April 26, 1934.

[65] For examples of these attacks, see John Flynn, "Other People's Money," *New Republic*, LXXXVIII (1936), 103–104; Margaret Marshall, "Columnists on Parade," *Nation*, CXLVI (1938), 464–67; and Barbara Giles, "Pundit in a Penthouse," *New Masses*, XXXVI (September 10, 1940), 11–12.

in the indictment. The real conflict, as Lippmann saw it, was not between the collectivist sects but between all forms of collectivism on one side and true liberalism on the other.

"True liberalism" was Lippmann's summary of the politics of the mature. It represented an attempt to find a way past both the spreading collectivism of the twentieth century and the smug satisfaction with the status quo which was so typical of the nineteenth. Involved was an emancipation of restraints upon the person of man in order to open up free science, the acceleration of invention, the liberation of the spirit, and the achievement of the "good life." Lippmann decisively rejected the notion that the state can authoritatively plan and impose the "good life" upon a great society.

But if men could not plan and direct society from above through the state, they could, thought Lippmann, provide for the careful administration of justice according to law. It was here that his thought in *The Good Society* took a notable step beyond *A Preface to Morals*. The earlier volume had, in somewhat cavalier fashion, disposed of tradition and most patterns of the past as having no valid function in the modern world. Pushed toward maturity by the pressures of a technological society, man (Lippmann had believed in 1929) could be depended upon at the least to maintain a basically intelligent structure of law and order. Since that writing, however, the world had watched the fires of totalitarianism begin to burn in Europe. By 1937 the Nazi "New Order" appeared increasingly malevolent. Throughout his career Lippmann's political proposals had rested on the assumption that so long as men operated under law, they could not swerve disastrously far from the legitimate ends of government. Now he had witnessed events which introduced unique factors. He had seen the liberal democracy of Germany's Weimar Republic commit legal suicide by voting away the people's liberties into the hands of Hitler and his cohorts. Without question, the National Socialists were the legally selected and functioning government of Germany; as such, however, they were using their position to turn the state into an arbitrary instrument of collectivist tyranny, seemingly with the consent of a majority of the German citizenry. Obviously, in the face of some threat such as Nazism, to parrot "government by law" was not sufficient. Other safeguards were required. Respect for law itself must be undergirded in some manner.

The Good Society showed the effect of this realization upon Lippmann. It is difficult to isolate the important influences which had altered his thinking, but they included a new respect for the heritage of Western civilization, and especially the development of common law. The ideas of the political theorist and historian Charles H. McIlwain appeared to play some role in the process, as did the writings of Dean Roscoe Pound of the Harvard Law School.[66] In addition, the thought of Edmund Burke, whom Lippmann had once charged with using political terms as useless as "inchoate lumps," had now assumed weight and meaning.[67]

In the final chapter of *The Good Society*, entitled "On This Rock," Lippmann articulated a prophetic development in his philosophical stance. He sought to penetrate behind human tradition—beyond even the Western heritage of constitutionalism and respect for law—seeking deeper roots and stronger foundations. Simple pragmatism was no longer sufficient, nor was the romantic naturalism of Santayana with its vague talk of unapproachable "essences." The long road that had begun for Walter Lippmann in his Harvard classrooms was taking a decisive turn in the direction of a "dim but powerful apprehension of some law higher than parliaments, majorities, or kings." [68]

On This Rock, 1938–55

In *A Preface to Politics*, written a quarter-century before *The Good Society*, Lippmann had decisively rejected any possibility of absolute, self-evident truths. In 1938 he refaced that question. "Per-

[66] See *The Good Society* (New York, 1937), 242–43, 318, 333, *passim*.
[67] Lippmann, "Vocabulary of Political Thought," *New Republic*, IV (1915), 24.
[68] Arthur M. Schlesinger, Jr., "Walter Lippmann: The Intellectual vs. Politics," in Childs and Reston (eds.), *Walter Lippmann and His Times*, 219.

haps in reasoning about the problem of our time," he wrote, "we have lost vital contact with the self-evident truths which have the capacity to infuse the longing to be civilized with universal and inexhaustible energy." What were these self-evident truths? Quite naturally, in the context of the lost liberties of much of mankind, Lippmann sought to find these truths in a determination "at what final rampart a man must stand when he fights for human freedom." The content of his answer was consistent with the pattern of his thought across the years, but his basis for this content sounded a new note. "The self-evident truth which makes men invincible is that undeniably they are inviolable persons." But how do men know that they are this kind of persons? "To the masses of the Western world the news that all men are more than things was proclaimed by the Christian gospel and was celebrated in its central mysteries. . . . Upon this rock . . . [men] have built the rude foundations of the Good Society." [69] With this remarkable declaration, Lippmann entered what appears to be the final and decisive stage of his pilgrimage.

World events delayed a fuller statement of the implications of this conclusion. While from 1931 to 1937 Lippmann felt free to devote the majority of his newspaper columns to domestic problems, after 1937 his attention was more and more fixed upon international affairs. As a result, the bulk of his writing—columns, articles, and books—dealt with this area. As early as 1938 he had begun to write the book which was to make more explicit the reliance upon natural law only hinted at in *The Good Society*. But, with the coming of World War II, he wrote, "I put the manuscript away, knowing that so much was going to happen to the world and to me that if I ever went back to the book, it would be to start all over again. When I did come back to it after the war, the foreboding which had inspired it was in a terrible manner realized." [70] The volume was finally published in 1955 as *The Public Philosophy*.

Sooner than most, Lippmann had seen the approaching maelstrom of war and its effect upon all of Western civilization.

[69] *The Good Society*, 372, 374, 378.
[70] *The Public Philosophy*, 13

During 1938, 1939, and 1940 he urged preparedness upon a re-luctant nation, seeking to bring Americans into a clearer under-standing of what the conflict with the totalitarians involved. In the presidential election of 1940 he was willing, for the sake of foreign policy, to lay aside his serious criticism of Franklin Roose-velt's domestic program. Throughout the war and afterwards, he gave himself to the pressing issues of foreign affairs, and his advice and insight gained increasing respect in Washington and across the world. Twice he visited the European theater of war and, on both occasions, he was received as a kind of unofficial special am-bassador by Winston Churchill and other European leaders.

Following his divorce from his first wife in 1937 and his remar-riage, Lippmann moved from New York to the nation's capital where his headquarters remained until 1967 (he has since re-turned to New York). Here, where he was in touch with government policy makers, his contact with officials was widespread. At times his stature was such that he was labeled a "one-man State Depart-ment," and one member of the policy planning staff of the Truman Administration's State Department has recalled that almost ev-ery meeting opened with a discussion of Lippmann's latest views.[71]

Recognition of Lippmann's standing and importance have come in varied ways. The honorary degrees he has accumulated from various colleges and universities may cause him to remember some-what wryly that he never took the time to finish a graduate degree at Harvard. His annual interviews on television have attracted wide attention. Two lengthy personal conversations with Nikita Khruschev have been published as significant books. A Pulitzer Prize for international reporting was awarded him in 1962, and shortly after his election John F. Kennedy came to call on Lipp-mann at his Washington home in order to counsel with him.

---

[71] Louis J. Halle, "Walter Lippmann," *New Republic*, CXLIX (1963), 20. This observation may, however, be taken with a grain of salt. In a con-versation with the author, another member of the policy planning staff, Charles Burton Marshall, commented, "That's easily explained. Halle al-ways brought up Lippmann, even when nobody else was interested."

Today Walter Lippmann is still active, still producing, still clarifying, still dredging up basic issues. In recent months he has devoted much of his writing to a critical analysis of American policy in Vietnam—a policy with which he decisively disagrees. On many matters of specific political controversy, one can find significant differences in the Lippmann of today from that one of fifty years ago, but these can be seen as the developing opinions of one who has never stopped learning. Much more significant is the gap which separates his fundamental political and philosophical stance today from that of 1913 and 1914. Even here, however, a remarkable line of continuity in purpose and emphasis can be traced from A *Preface to Politics* to *The Public Philosophy*. The Lippmann of today seems as certain as when he sat in Graham Wallas' classes that no political theory can afford to ignore the human personality—the whole person. But he has learned a great deal about the makeup of that whole person across the years, and what he has learned has stamped and shaped his entire philosophy. Once he turned his back upon the past; now he seeks to draw from it a respect for the "traditions of civility"—the heritage of Western man.

His intellectual pilgrimage has issued in a unique blending of past and present, a major attempt to correlate contemporary empirical analysis with the hard-won traditional wisdom of the human race. To uncover the self-understanding upon which this philosophy rests is the task to which we now turn.

"How hard it is to find anything you can love," I complained. "What do you love, Walter?" "The living world," he answered.

MABEL DODGE LUHAN

Chapter II

The Nature of Man

The virtual truism that one's political philosophy is intimately linked with his concept of man has been tersely put by George Peabody Gooch: "Our political ideas are determined in a last resort by the estimate we have formed of human nature." [1] An understanding of the politics of Walter Lippmann requires, however, the additional dimension of a distinctive kind of personalism. The Lippmann approach rests not simply upon his concept of men's nature but also upon a fundamental value judgment—namely that, in the world as we know it, *man as a living person* occupies first place in the value hierarchy. From *A Preface to Politics*, with its reiteration of Graham Wallas' call for the application of modern psychology to political theory, to *The Public Philosophy*, with its presupposition of the value of man as a spiritual entity, the centrality of the person is the key to Lippmann's approach. His theoretical writings fall into coherent sequence only when viewed as continuing, flexible attempts to validate the integrity of the person and to analyze the problems of political society in terms of that validation.

[1] Cited in Newton D. Baker, "The Good Society of the Future," *Atlantic*, CLX (1937), 612.

No abrupt changes mark the pattern of this development; rather it can be graphed as a gradual movement away from a somewhat naive, self-centered assumption of the worth of personality toward a far more sophisticated and carefully worked out stance. The movement has been informed by a conscious realization of the necessity for value structures originating outside the individual human being to sustain man's inner sense of dignity. In a striking manner this pattern reflects the intellectual and philosophical flux in which Lippmann has lived, by which he has been influenced, and to which he has contributed.

To understand Lippmann's thought in this area it helps to center upon certain major works in which the developing stages of his conception of human nature are most clearly expressed. He himself has suggested that the significant milestones are *A Preface to Politics* (1913), *A Preface to Morals* (1929), *The Good Society* (1937), and *The Public Philosophy* (1955).[2] While complex concepts always evolve slowly and cannot be separated into exclusive classifications, the task of understanding will be simplified if Lippmann's ideas are viewed under four rough categories: (1) the irrational man; (2) the disinterested man; (3) the liberal man; and (4) the civilized man. These categories are not intended to be totally parallel; in Lippmann's thought some are descriptive, others prescriptive.

The Irrational Man

Lippmann's contemporary portrait of man is clearly visualized only against the background of his starting point. Virtually all the ingredients of his more mature conceptions were present, at least seminally, in the beginning, but the proportions of the mixture and the emphasis given to each element have changed markedly in the course of the years. Dominating his thought in the days prior to World War II was an image typical of the age. Most readily

[2] Cited in William D. Muller, "An Interpretation of the Political Philosophy of Walter Lippmann: The Nature of Man" (Typescript in Lippmann Collection, Yale University Library), 1.

available in his first major book, A *Preface to Politics*, its constituent elements were drawn largely from William James, Sigmund Freud, Graham Wallas, and Henri Bergson. Each thinker from his distinctive perspective had challenged the prevailing mechanistic theories of sociologist Herbert Spencer and his disciples, with their insistence on rigid laws of social development and change. To Lippmann and many of his contemporaries, Spencer's "pretentious general formulation of the necessary conduct of men in society" seemed unrealistic, lacking in sensitivity, and without insight into the dynamics of human existence.[3] As young men, they were part of the continuing intellectual ferment which had first been stirred by the publication of Lester F. Ward's watershed volume, *Dynamic Sociology*. Influenced by such thought, they could not conceive of man's behavior in society as being mechanically subject to external forces in the same manner as physical bodies. Life was an evolving process, full of individual variations, concerned not only with facts but also with subjective human values. Above all, society reflected the freedom of men who envisaged ideals, communicated them to others, and invented ways to implement them. The hero of the scheme was the creative social engineer who brought technical resources for achievement to the service of realistic social ideals.

At the center of every social analysis is a selected normative example of the human being; Lippmann's norm was the "deliberate, conscious, willing individual," and at this stage of his thought, the emphasis was decisively on "willing." Such a man is prisoner neither of his environment nor of classic social laws. He is free—a "mover and shaker"—capable, at least potentially, of manipulating the world about him to fit his purposes. A central key to understanding man, argued Lippmann, is "this power of being aggressively active toward the world," a power which assures man "that the world is something he can make."[4]

Lippmann was not merely calling up again the image of the

[3] Herbert Croly, "Introduction" in E. C. Lindeman, *Social Discovery* (New York, 1925), xiii.
[4] A *Preface to Politics*, 9, 12.

eighteenth century's calm man of reason, progressively uncovering by the methods of logic and science the secrets of a self-contained nature. On the contrary, Lippmann's man was a complex bundle of drives, passions, and instincts. True, he was a thinker, capable of employing reason as well as the experimental techniques of science, but he deceived himself if he ever believed that either he or any of his fellows was directed by a pure, objective rationality. Reason, as Lippmann conceived it, ultimately functions as the servant of irrationality. For substantiation, he pointed back to the Scottish skeptic David Hume, who had discovered that "reason itself is an irrational impulse." [5] Properly understood as a tool, rationality is invaluable to man in the selection of means to reach desired ends, but the ends themselves cannot be conceived as reasonable. Rather, they derive from the deepest inner instincts of mankind. Reason is enlisted in the service of will, and will, finally, is the slave of passionate drives.

Any promising source of light upon the nature of these inner drives must partake strongly of introspection, thought Lippmann, and he enthusiastically welcomed the researches of Sigmund Freud, whom he saw as documenting the ideas implicit in the thought of James and Wallas. "The impetus of Freud is perhaps the greatest advance ever made toward the understanding and control of human characters," he wrote.[6] But Freud's study, promising as it was, had not progressed far enough, and Lippmann realized that knowledge in this area was still fragmentary. Even so (and here, the pragmatic calls to action of William James became important), the practice of politics could not await Freud's arrival at definitive results. Men must move ahead boldly on the basis of what they did know about human nature. Unless it sought consciously to adapt itself to the needs evidenced by basic human

[5] *Ibid.*, 215. In an earlier work Lippmann had quoted Graham Wallas approvingly: "In order to make men think, one must begin by making them feel." See Lippmann, "In Defense of the Suffragettes," *Harvard Monthly*, XIX (November, 1909), 64.

[6] *A Preface to Politics*, 68. In a letter to Justice Oliver Wendell Holmes, dated November 29, 1916, Harold Laski commented: "I wish Lippmann would forget Freud for a little—just a little." See Mark DeWolfe Howe (ed.), *The Holmes–Laski Letters* (Cambridge, 1953), I, 36.

desires, no theory of politics was acceptable. Indeed, the role of government could be summed up as the provision of practical avenues for the constructive fulfillment of these desires.

What Lippmann believed was that men's instinctive, irrational desires are primitive keys to the true, legitimate needs and ends of human personality. To understand man, one must first of all comprehend his needs; and to create a good society, political efforts must be directed toward the satisfaction of these needs. Lippmann did not try to deal with problems arising from the fact that human impulses and legitimate human interests often are in conflict. The decisive questions of how and whether the vast diversity of individual human interests could actually be welded into a cohesive social purpose was largely ignored. He assumed that men's individual desires—freely, naturally, and constructively expressed —could be made to fall into a social harmony.

The impossibility of effectively denying or repressing man's instincts strongly impressed Lippmann. If not constructively released, these drives burst forth in other ways that cause dislocation and pain for the individual and for society. The attempt to suppress or inhibit them by law is worse than useless; it is deformative and productive of even more destructive consequences. To "taboo" liquor or prostitution, for instance, is a foolish evasion of the problem. Men drink or patronize prostitutes as the expression of their basic humanity. Instead of barring these outlets, the government should provide more satisfactory alternatives—"moral equivalents," Lippmann called them, in imitation of William James. In fact, he asserted in an all-embracing and optimistic statement, "The assumption is that every lust is capable of some civilized expression." [7]

Implicit in this anthropology is a conception of evil as an undesirable manifestation of man's basic impulses. Lippmann made this definition explicit when he described evil simply as an alternative and inferior way of expression. Far from being inevitable sources of sin, man's "rooted lusts" contain the dynamics of human character. Only as a particular mode of expression produces

[7] A Preface to Politics, 50.

pain or social dislocation can it—the outlet, not the drive itself—
be classified as evil. From this perspective, empirical man can in
no sense be called inherently bad. Though endowed with the irrational power of instinctive desire, he is morally neutral. As Lippmann saw it, the degree to which desire is fulfilled in a socially
constructive and personally satisfying way is the only allowable
standard of virtue. When society makes such outlets possible, it
converts the natural human thrust into the raw material of unlimited potential for good.

So enthusiastically did Lippmann propound the endless possibilities of human progress that it is not difficult to understand
how his English friend Harold Laski misjudged his outlook. In a
letter to Justice Oliver Wendell Holmes in 1916, Laski wrote, "I
am a Darwinian and Croly, Lippmann, *et al*, seem to me really theologians—for they believe either in goodness or in sin as original
and they have what I take to be a pathetic trust in environmental
change." [8] Others have since echoed Laski's estimate, but it must
be emphasized that at this point Lippmann did not intend to pass
judgment on the goodness or badness of man's essential nature.
The nature of man is there; it must be recognized and understood,
not morally evaluated. What matters (and, again, Lippmann's
pragmatic underpinnings were showing) is the consequence of expressing this nature.

Laski's second criticism—that of trust in environment—had
more validity, though not exactly in the manner in which he understood it. Lippmann's mistake was not really that of believing
over-strongly in the power of environment to alter basic human
nature. Because he saw man not as isolated or atomistic but as
social, he judged the social manifestations of his nature to be mal-
leable, almost without limit.[9] Institutions, education, and the
constructs of society can provide progressively more satisfactory

[8] Howe (ed.), *The Holmes–Laski Letters*, I, 17. The letter is dated
September 9, 1916.
[9] For a discussion of this aspect of Lippmann's thought, see David W.
Noble, "The *New Republic* and the Idea of Progress, 1914–20," *Mississippi
Valley Historical Review*, XXXVIII (1951), 387–402.

means of channeling man's passions. In its essence, however, human nature changes extremely slowly, if at all, and is beyond the effective reach of man's manipulation. Only the ways in which that nature expresses itself can be shaped.

Lippmann's real problem was not that he trusted environment too much, but rather that he placed his confidence in an almost wholly autonomous individual whose goals and ends are irrationally dictated. He saw man's distinguishing mark as his freedom of will, and he sought to extricate the individual from the trappings of the past, which no longer concern him, and to make him unchallenged master of the future. No transcendental dimensions hamper such a man, and no absolutes bind him, for, as Nietzsche had discovered, each individual creates his own values. Subject to no limitations (as far as ultimate goals are concerned) except the amorphous forces of his own undefined instinctual urges, man, thought Lippmann, can be trusted to take the powerful instruments of technology and science in hand and build a better world. In the exciting atmosphere of pre-World War I, such a faith did not appear to be wholly unrealistic.

Even the heady optimism of that age, however, would not allow Lippmann entirely to ignore concrete experience. Lincoln Steffens had taught him the peril of disregarding facts, and the facts of the human situation demonstrated to Lippmann that, in politics as everywhere else, some men are more capable of constructive expression than others. From this recognition rose a significant doctrine of the elite—one which was, in varying forms, to remain a persistent element in his thought. Men possess infinite variety. Any realistic political theory has to take these variations into acute consideration, rather than to make the mistake, in Macaulay's terms, of the tailor who measured the clothes of all his customers by the Apollo Belvedere. For instance, while sharing a common fund of instinct, men differ markedly in the strength of their drives. They also differ in their degree of rational competence and training. Thus, as both observation and reflection demonstrate, men divide themselves naturally into certain broad categories— classes which are fluid rather than fixed, but at any one moment, largely determinable. Most men fall into the great group called the "mass," those who operate in life and politics with a relative minimum of knowledge and rationality. Their chief guides to choice are the uncritical acceptance of tradition and the unrefined satisfaction of their impulses. In this regard, Lippmann echoed the conclusions of his teacher Graham Wallas, one of whose themes was that most men do not rationally calculate ends and then select means designed to reach those ends. Man's instinctive needs provide the ends; therefore, the political problem lies in the selection of proper means. Who is to lead in this kind of political action?

Under the scheme of human nature to which he was committed, Lippmann necessarily relied on an elite of particularly qualified and gifted men. The idea that all men can move cooperatively toward political ends without the aid of naturally qualified leaders —a contention which Lippmann somewhat contemptuously identified with orthodox socialism[10]—is a delusion. Since any social movement demands leadership and can move only so far as its leaders project it, the instincts of the common man require the creative touch of a leader who understands them.

In *A Preface to Politics* Lippmann separated the elite into two sections. The larger but subordinate class (later to be given much more prominence) consisted of technically qualified, scientifically trained experts. Despite their advantages, however, these men are still limited, for they tend to become prisoners of over-intellectualization and unimaginative education. Even so brilliant a thinker as Woodrow Wilson displayed the characteristic weaknesses, for Lippmann at first doubted that his "imagination was fibrous enough to catch the inwardness of the mutterings" of the age.[11]

Within his elite Lippmann discovered an upper echelon, a small minority of leaders whom he termed statesmen. Of this type Theodore Roosevelt was his prime example. The statesman (or "inventor," as Lippmann also called him) applies to his task of leadership more than the resources of reason and science. He brings to

[10] Cf. A *Preface to Politics*, 16.
[11] *Ibid.*, 302.

it a certain creative intuitiveness, in Bergson's sense. Such a statesman begins by accepting human nature. He makes no value judgments on it, nor does he concern himself with whether it can be
changed. Rather, he seeks to sense the thrust of mass human desires and to provide healthy opportunities for the expression of
human impulses. He serves as an intermediary and catalyst, bringing
together trained social engineers and the constituency of the masses.
In effect, he is an expert at choosing experts. As Lippmann glow-
ingly described him, he "makes social movements conscious
of themselves, expresses their needs, gathers their power, then
thrusts them behind the inventor and the technicians in the task
of actual achievement." [12] Lippmann had great faith in his statesmen, and he harnessed his own career to those he judged to fit
this category.

In summary, the irrational man, as Lippmann saw him, is instinctual, creative, and manipulative of his environment. He operates, as did Lippmann himself at this time, from the presupposition that the human personality in its raw potential stands at
the center of the universe; therefore, the purpose of all worthwhile effort is to fulfill man's needs. The normative man does not
rationally substantiate this conviction. He simply "feels" it to be
true. But while this whole concept of human nature was thoroughly optimistic, it was not identical with the naive and idealistic
commitment of many of Lippmann's fellows who saw only good in
the human being and consistently idealized the masses. The difference came through most clearly in *Drift and Mastery*, the book
which quickly followed *A Preface to Politics*. Here, Lippmann
analyzed the American temperament as leaning toward a sort of
"mystical anarchism, in which the 'natural' humanity in each man
is adored as the savior of society." [13]

With all his talk of freedom for impulses, Lippmann's acute
empirical perception made him unable to put complete trust in
the unsophisticated man or to posit any ultimate human goodness. "Human nature," he commented, "is a rather shocking affair

[12] *Ibid.*
[13] *Drift and Mastery*, 177.

if you come to it with ordinary romantic optimism." [14] Even at
this early state in his career, his capacity to maintain a degree of
intellectual balance and detachment tended to curb Lippmann's
enthusiasm and made him, by contrast with many of his contemporaries, seem cold and uninvolved. His insistence on the need for
elite leadership reflected a basic distrust of mass competence. Perhaps it was this stubborn feature of Lippmann's thought which
so irritated some of his Greenwich Village friends. Hutchins Hap-
good, for instance, once wrote to Mabel Dodge Luhan: "If you
sometimes will go down to the Bowery and see the Booze victims,
you will see another way in which God manifests himself. God
doesn't manifest himself *at all* in Walter Lippmann." [15]

The Disinterested Man

From A *Preface to Politics* to A *Preface to Morals* is a major
leap, particularly in regard to Lippmann's concept of man. Some
mention must be made, therefore, of the principal elements of
change which seem to have entered into his thinking during the
intervening sixteen years.

Dependence on the statesman as an "elite of the elite" appears
to have been the first major casualty of his early thought. As already indicated, Lippmann's disillusionment with Theodore Roosevelt, followed by a rather traumatic loss of confidence in Woodrow Wilson, helped produce this effect. Intuitive, creative leadership failed to measure up to his high hopes, and as early as
1914, in *Drift and Mastery*, he was shifting his allegiance more
completely to the experts—the objective, scientific minds who
can uncover facts, weigh consequences, and devise techniques for
action. Lippmann's thinking during the first years of World War
I was partly influenced by John Dewey, who was calling for "free
and effectively organized intelligence" as the answer to all the
problems of society. Reviewing Dewey's *Education and Democracy*, Lippmann termed the philosopher-educator "the first and

[14] A *Preface to Politics*, 39.
[15] Luhan, *Movers and Shakers*, 487.

most powerful intellect devoted to the future of American civilization" and went on to give unqualified endorsement to Dewey's
ideas on education as "the best hope of liberal man." [16]

Obviously, the direction of shift in Lippmann's picture of man
was in the direction of a greater emphasis on rationality. Still, this
conception could be achieved for him, in the face of the hard facts
of human existence, only through the accentuation of his idea of
the elite. As Lippmann increased his expectations of what the
expert could accomplish in society, he perceived more clearly, under the shocks of World War I plus the superficial extremes of the
1920's, the basic conflict between rational and irrational factors
in human nature. He was impelled by his propaganda experience in
the war and his studies of news distortion at the turn of the
decade to put more and more dependence on education and the
scientific method. By the time he wrote *Public Opinion* in 1922
his psychological understanding of man had entered a new and
distinctly Platonic stage. Men, he still thought, are largely bound
by their irrationality, but for this condition there is a discernible
reason. They do not comprehend objective truth for they are
still in the shadows of the cave. Not accurate understanding, but
"stereotypes" —"pictures in men's minds"—are the real spurts to
action. And, for the great mass, this situation is unavoidable. So
complex has life become that few men have the chance to see anything clearly beyond the limited context of their own narrow personal interests. The larger world is mediated to them along avenues
of information and communication, and only as these agencies of
information are manned by clear-thinking, impartial scientists
can the public depend upon them. Thus, *Public Opinion* broad-
ened the gap between the irrational common man and the expert,
a gap that became even more pronounced in *The Phantom Public*
(1924), in which Lippmann concluded that the public could not,
even through the use of scientifically operated intelligence agencies,
gain sufficient knowledge and insight to enable them to determine
complicated government policy. The best they can do, thought

[16] Lippmann, "The Hope of Democracy," *New Republic*, VII (1916),
231.

Lippmann, struggling to maintain a justification for democratic government by consent, is at regular intervals to choose good leaders who can be trusted to devise and administer wise policy.

In the middle twenties, then, Lippmann was hard put to maintain a tenuous connection between the irrational mass and the scientific elite. He sought to do so by contending that, despite their limitations, all men are susceptible to a degree of rational development and of response to rational leadership. Man is at least potentially reasonable, though only a select few achieve a dependable measure of full rationality. On these few the remainder must rely for guidance.

While this theory dealt directly with the choosing of means and methods in political society (a rational process, as Lippmann had always maintained), it left unanswered the crucial problem of the selection of ends. In A *Preface to Politics* he had been willing to leave these ends to the natural thrust of human drives; his later experience and deeper reflection had shaken this confidence. How then would ends be chosen? In what ultimate directions should human society seek to move?

The attempt to deal with this troubling issue produced A *Preface to Morals* and, in the process, propelled Lippmann even more drastically in the direction of a special kind of aesthetic rationalism, similar in many ways to the thought of his teacher Santayana. Still aware of the explosive nature of man's instinctive impulses, he was ready now to assert that a man's higher nature—including both the capacity for reason and the sense of artistic appreciation —has power to tame the irrational thrusts. His counsel was no longer the "express yourself" of the halcyon days before World War I, but rather, "control yourself." By this he did not propose the rigid kind of unenlightened aesceticism which he identified generally with Christianity, but instead an intelligent, civilized stoicism by which man taught himself to desire only those things which he could realistically have. In this manner, Lippmann thought, men could achieve the twin goals of harmony and happiness.

The selection of life's ends had now become for Lippmann an intellectual and aesthetic process. He had moved far from William James's insistence on some sort of intuitive estimate of goals toward Santayana's dictum that the will must be enlisted in the service of reason, instead of primitive feeling. The process by which this was accomplished Lippmann described as the passage from childishness to maturity. Psychologizing human nature in a different way from that of 1913, though with clear lines of connection to that earlier concept, he defined childishness as the domination of man by his primal desires, and maturity as the refinement and adjustment of those desires in the light of man's recognition of reality. This mature person he called "the disinterested man."

Lippmann saw the disinterested man as having rationally divested himself of any illusions as to the nature of the universe. There is no transcendental system of values, no "Friend behind phenomena"; the universe is neither friendly nor unfriendly. It is as it is, and must be faced in that way. Just as in A *Preface to Politics* Lippmann had argued that human nature is *there*, now he asserted that the objective world is *there*. Since ultimate circumstances cannot be altered, the secret of overcoming such elements of experience as pain, suffering, disappointment, or evil is individual and subjective. "The realization that evil exists only because we feel it to be painful helps us not only to dissociate it from this aura of dread but to dissociate ourselves from our own feelings about it. This is a momentous achievement in the inner life of man." Men learn to be satisfied with the things they would want "if they knew what they were doing," and are then mature.[17]

No doubt this kind of maturity is a difficult achievement. Indeed, Lippmann admitted that it "has, in all ages, seemed so unapproachably high that it has been reserved for a voluntary aristocracy of the spirit."[18] But, he argued, as his still-strong strain of optimism showed itself, the urgent and unparalleled need for this

[17] A *Preface to Morals*, 219, 319.
[18] *Ibid.*, 203.

philosophy under the strains of modern life is itself a prophecy. What had been a spiritual luxury for the few must now become the possession of the many, and *what is needed so desperately will be.*

The question of *how* it will be opened up some of the ambiguities in Lippmann's thought. He had reduced man's problem to a largely subjective one. He had lost much of his confidence in the directional drive of man's natural impulses. He had conceded the practical unchangeableness of the hard core of human nature. Yet now he fell back upon an almost inevitable, institutionalized, intellectualized force which was going to shape human beings— more or less, sooner or later—into mature, disinterested men caught up in the high, humanistic "religion of the spirit." His miracle-working force—"the creative principle in modernity"—was science which, by its detached and objective methodology, was rapidly transforming every area of life. Pure science, thought Lippmann, is "high religion incarnate," and at the heart of modern civilization it is bringing into play motives and habits of mind which are mature and disinterested.[19] To illustrate his point, Lippmann took three chapters in *A Preface to Morals* to deal with practical problems, and in the realms of business, government, and sexual mores he sought to demonstrate the power of scientific, disinterested thinking to modify man's life. What Lippmann was asserting was that technological society has a built-in solution to its own problems; not only that, but modern life operates so as virtually to force the acceptance of that solution. While man's distinctive mark is his freedom, expressed in terms of voluntary choice, he is also made so that he requires authority and guidance for his actions. The acids of modernity have erased traditional moral and religious sources of authority beyond restoration, but this same modernity is pushing man into a healthy, mature reliance upon his own innate authority, embodied in an objective, detached, scientific mind. Once human freedom is united with the autonomous authority of the disinterested man, human beings are mature. "Modern civilization requires science; science develops rationality;

[19] *Ibid.,* 237–39.

civilization will become rational!" [20] It was a neat and heartening scheme.

Such was Walter Lippmann's portrait of the disinterested man and his world. Painted with skill in the pages of *A Preface to Morals*, it had much to recommend it to frustrated, uprooted, confused men and women. Each reader tended to see himself as fully capable of and, perhaps, well on the way toward becoming one of Lippmann's elite of mature individuals. Little wonder the book found a hearing. It was a Book-of-the-Month Club selection and a best-seller. Nevertheless, its picture of man, despite its urbane charm, left decisive questions unanswered.

In the light of historical events, Lippmann himself was to realize that his concept of man had taken the power of evil too lightly, handling it glibly as something the individual could subjectively control. But even this obvious criticism of the disinterested man does not reach the core of the trouble. With all his dignity and courageous realism, Lippmann's mature individual was but a half-man. Despite much talk of the centuries-old traditions of "high religion," he was effectively cut off, not only from history and the accumulated spiritual experience of men, but also from the contemporary human community. He lived in society, not because he was by nature a social being, but because circumstances forced him to do so. So individualized was the disinterested man, in the last analysis, that the dimensions of fellowship had become virtually meaningless. Little real consideration was given to man's inescapable connections with and obligations to community. Evidence of this deficiency was found in the closing statement of *A Preface to Morals*, previously quoted. Only a half-man, overly subjectivized, an isolated, barricaded island in the sea of humanity, could be pictured as observing the unrolling panorama of experience—not only his own but that of other men as well—with the attitude attributed to him by Lippmann. Regardless of how much

[20] Charles E. Schutz, "The Development and Significance of the Political Thought of Walter Lippmann" (Ph.D. dissertation, University of Chicago, 1962), 284.

pain and suffering that experience might include, the mature man, by Lippmann's definition, "whether he saw the thing as comedy, or high tragedy, or farce . . . ," [21] could *enjoy* it. The hard question remained: should men, or perhaps better, could real men turn real life into a theatrical performance, with themselves as detached spectators?

The Liberal Man

The striking amount of difference which exists between the irrational man of Walter Lippmann's 1913 thought and the disinterested man he described in 1929 is not apparent when one comes to the picture of the true liberal, delineated most clearly in *The Good Society* (1937). Lippmann's basic concept of human nature changed little during the eight years from 1929 to 1937. Significantly, however, certain implications of his earlier views became more apparent, requiring adjustments of thought and raising difficult problems.

In this period Lippmann was primarily concerned with determining the kind of political order demanded by his conception of man's nature. His search for a "politics of disinterest" led him to support a type of governmental arrangement in which mature men, jealous of their freedom and individuality, could function most effectively. He found his model in the "true liberalism" of Adam Smith and the eighteenth century progressives—a liberalism which he felt had been corrupted by its unfortunate confusion with a continuing policy of political and economic laissez faire and which had grown decadent and reactionary by the latter half of the nineteenth century. True liberalism united two political fundamentals, both of which were essential to Lippmann: first, *limited government,* so as to insure increasing freedom for the individual by the removal of as many restraints as possible; and second, *dynamic government,* which, though conscious of its limits, did not hesitate to intervene aggressively in society when-

[21] *A Preface to Morals,* 330.

ever and wherever circumstances hindered genuine freedom and competitive opportunity for any citizen.

Thus, in the political area, Lippmann visualized his normative man as a responsible, mature individual, insisting on equal opportunities for all and achieving the upper limits of his creative potential. He rejected all forms of state collectivism, insisting that "the road whereby mankind has advanced in knowledge, in the mastery of nature, in unity, and in personal security has lain through a progressive emancipation from the bondage of authority. . . ." [22] His ideal was eloquently expressed in a beautiful tribute he wrote to the social reformer Jane Addams.

That . . . is why those who have known her say that she was not only good but great. For this blend of sympathy with distinction, of common humanity with a noble style, is recognizable by those who have eyes to see it as the occasional but authentic issue of the mystic promise of the American democracy. It is the quality which reached its highest expression in Lincoln. . . . This is the ultimate vindication of the democratic faith, not that men may be brought to a common level, but that without pomp or pride or power or privilege, every man might and some men will achieve again and again the highest possibilities of the human spirit.[23]

Lippmann was developing a train of thought which had its roots in his earliest conviction of the value of human personality. Government has no right to collectivize men, for this demeaned free men by treating them as things. True, man was no longer the morally neutral, instinctively productive being of A Preface to Politics, ideally capable of mastering every phase of his environment; he was, potentially at least, a rational and aesthetically-oriented stoic who found happiness through adjusting himself to the unalterable patterns of a neutral universe. But his prime value had not changed. The human person was still paramount, and government was required to respect that person.

By 1937, however, two crucial and complicating considerations

[22] The Good Society, 19.
[23] "Today and Tomorrow," May 23, 1935.

had invaded Lippmann's thought. The second arose from the first, and both disturbed the calm logic of his system.

One was Lippmann's increasing awareness of something he had rather easily disposed of, both in 1913 and in 1929: the force of evil, which now seemed to him to have entrenched itself much more doggedly in the human personality than he had previously realized. Looking back at the pre-World War I days, Lippmann recalled, "We had grown up in an era of peace and we had no idea how men behave when their customary way of life is disrupted and their familiar habits are disordered. We had no idea of how fragile are the bonds of a civilized existence." [24] Two events in history had dramatically revealed dark dimensions of the human personality. One was the world-wide depression of the early thirties, during which Lippmann had observed men who had lost their economic security willingly sell their freedom and self-respect—the distinctive characteristics, he thought, of a human being—for bread. The other and even more compelling demonstration was the rise of a brutal, cruel, and unbelievably inhuman totalitarianism in one of the most civilized nations on earth, Germany.

These events forced Lippmann to put new emphasis on such elements in man as the necessity for security and the lust for power. "My observation," he wrote, "is that the human craving for power is insatiable and that it grows by what it feeds upon." [25] He saw new significance in the long experience of mankind with the corruption of personal power, and he had come to the conclusion that man's vaunted virtue and culture are, too often, merely superficial coverings for inestimable evil and far too frail to effectively restrain men's passions. "One of the few things we know with reasonable certainty is that there is no sharp dividing line between those who may commit crimes and those who will not commit them. . . . The best of us is only a recently and partially civilized barbarian." [26]

[24] Lippmann, "Loud-Mouthed Barbarians," *Vital Speeches of the Day*, III (1937), 587.
[25] "Today and Tomorrow," February 17, 1937.
[26] *Ibid.*, July 3, 1937.

If evil in mankind is far more dangerous, unpredictable, and un-controllable than he had heretofore recognized,[27] another reality consequently presented itself—the inevitable limitations of men, all men, even Lippmann's elite of disinterested liberals.[28] In the light of this realization he found himself arguing against govern-mental collectivism and planned economy, because no man or group of men can finally be trusted to organize the total life of a nation. "It makes no difference," he wrote, "whether the rulers of a state inherit authority or were elected to it, whether they re-ceived it by appointment or have captured it by force; it makes no difference where they came from or how they are thought to be inspired or to what grandeur or glory they aspire. They are men, and so their powers are limited." [29]

The unhindered power to rule, exercised by men of limited minds and self-regarding prejudices, is certain to become oppres-sive, reactionary, and corrupt. To expect otherwise is to expect "more intelligence, more discipline, more disinterestedness, than exists in any ordinary company of men." [30] To trade one's liberty for the hope of economic security in collectivism is to sell one's birthright for a particularly unsavory mess of pottage.

Thus, Lippmann found himself confronted with a dilemma rooted in his concept of human nature. Man is supremely im-portant; he is, in fact, an "inviolable person." If government ful-fills its rightful purpose, those in places of authority must recog-nize this personal value. Government must be restrained from acting arbitrarily, from treating men like things. Yet, those who administer governments are themselves limited men with inher-ent potential for evil. Even those mature, disinterested men on

[27] Of his earlier views Lippmann wrote in 1937: "We were, it seems to me, now as I look back on it, like the peasants who move about drowsily in the sun on the slopes of Mt. Vesuvius, unable to realize the forces pent up within the volcano. We thought all the volcanoes were extinct." See "Loud-Mouthed Barbarians," 587.

[28] "Perhaps in a world made lunatic by self-appointed messiahs, such a sense of the limitations of men is the beginning of wisdom." See "Today and Tomorrow," January 1, 1938.

[29] The Good Society, 24.

[30] Ibid., 40.

whom Lippmann had pinned his earlier hopes are susceptible to temptation, especially the lust for power and self-aggrandizement. And there is no guarantee that the masses themselves under a democratic regime will not bargain away their own freedoms. The gap between the elite and the masses, a continuing substance of Lippmann's thought, thus lost much of its meaning. What is required is some *external* restraint upon all men, since autonomous rationality has proved itself insufficient. "Logical analysis cannot anticipate what the human will is likely to make of the situation in which it finds itself." [31] In the complexities of modern life amorphous freedom has demonstrated its inadequacy; man requires order and certainty as well as freedom, and for his fulfillment this order must arise out of some structure of reality beyond his own final control, else he will continually misshape and deform the patterns.

In *The Good Society* Lippmann was prepared to set out only the broadest possible answer to this dilemma. He insisted that the great bulwark of protection for the inviolable person is the Western heritage of common law—a method of governing which rules out arbitrary treatment. He still echoed a phase of his earliest thought, insisting that there exists in all men an instinct for self-government. But he had seen enough to convince him that no simple reliance on the rationality expressed in legal rules of procedure, much less on instinct, is a final solution. Pushed back past propositions he had previously assumed to be self-evident, he faced the fundamental questions: why is man's person inviolable? What is the ultimate validation of a nonarbitrary system of law?

Lippmann sought to state his answer in the closing pages of his book, but he appeared to be still so unused to it himself as to prevent any genuine development of its implications. The conviction that man is an inviolable person of worth and value, he said, has religious roots. "For in the recognition that there is in each man a final essence—that is to say, an immortal soul—which only God can judge, a limit was set upon the dominion of man over

[31] *American Inquisitors* (New York, 1928), 116–17.

man." [32] This is the rock upon which the foundations of the good society have been constructed. Out of this religious assertion has evolved the political, legal, and moral heritage of Western civilization. The common law tradition is but one expression of a "higher law"—a law taking precedence over all else, which insists that men created by God are free persons and must be so treated. All earthly political structures must be judged by this law, and only in it can man find his necessary order and authority.

The Civilized Man

Walter Lippmann's contemporary understanding of man undergirds *The Public Philosophy*, published in 1955. The concept of human nature which is presupposed in this volume grows out of the propositions set forth in the final sections of *The Good Society* and represents a logical development of that trend of thought.

Throughout his career, Lippmann has been troubled by the ambiguous character of human nature and the resulting tensions between the rational and irrational factors within that nature. In his early thought he attempted to resolve the tension by predicating man as essentially instinctive; for this kind of man, reason occupied the status of a valuable tool for the achievement rather than the selection of ends. Later, he inclined strongly toward the rational aspects of human nature, and in *A Preface to Morals* he proclaimed the ideal man to be one who had achieved self-mastery of the primitive forces and drives within his own nature by the application of an aesthetic type of reason which deliberately altered the ends of life in the interest of harmony and realism. By the time *The Good Society* was written, experience and world events had forced Lippmann to reevaluate the power and universality of the irrational forces in man. Accordingly, he once more questioned the ability of man's reason to completely subdue and control them.

Parallel to this dual quality in his conception of man's inner be-

[32] *The Good Society*, 378.

ing, Lippmann was constructing a corresponding duality in society as a whole. In the early years he posited an elite which included those who intuitively sensed the true thrust of man's instinctive nature, an understanding which the masses did not possess. Later, the character of the elite took on a more intellectual cast, even as his idea of the separation within man's nature between the rational and irrational forces sharpened. The objective, scientific experts of the early 1920's obviously corresponded, in a social sense, to the rational side of man's individual nature, and the mature, disinterested man of A *Preface to Morals* represented the ultimate triumph of this aspect of human makeup.

After 1929 Lippmann found it more and more difficult to maintain the integrity of his concept of the elite. He began to see that his division of human beings broke down into thoroughly artificial categories. The purely disinterested man was a Lippmann legend. Flesh-and-blood leaders, even though philosophically and aesthetically trained and disciplined, proved by their inadequate and often destructive action the continuing power of the inner human conflict.

As a result Lippmann, especially after 1937, centered his thought less upon an empirical elite in society and more upon the internal struggle which involves all men alike. Thus, in *The Public Philosophy*, his discussion revolved around a concept of reality as involving two realms of being—essence and existence—while, correspondingly, man is seen as possessing two natures: the natural or uncivilized self, which is basically irrational and represents the realm of existence; and the civilized or rational self, which finds its congenial environment in the realm of essence. In "the traditions of civility" (the term Lippmann uses to denote what he takes to be the mainstream of the Western tradition), "man's second and more rational nature must master his first and more elemental." [33]

Certainly, this understanding was not born full-grown. As early as 1942, in an address to the American Catholic Philosophical Association, Lippmann had set out a skeleton of his view. He had

[33] *The Public Philosophy*, 71.

argued then that the modern world's sickness had its roots in its image of man, which held that in human nature desire is sovereign, while reason is only the instrument for serving and satisfying desire. He thus condemned a version of man somewhat allied to his own early understanding. The true picture of man, he now contended, is "that man is so constituted that his greatest need is not the satisfaction of his desires but that his reason shall impose law and order upon his desires." [34]

The concept of two realms is basic to Lippmann's present thought. The first realm, that of *existence,* is identified with the arena of this world in which the human condition is to be born, to live, to work, to struggle, and to die. It is the realm of sense experience, of ambiguity, of frustration. Within it no reform can ever completely succeed, no good ambition be fully realized, no society achieve ultimate justice, freedom, or order. It is the dwelling place of man's first nature, his fallen self, of which the prime infection is "the moral sin original"—the delusion of men that they are gods and that they can construct a heaven on earth. [35] Here, believes Lippmann, is the great evil of totalitarianism. Both the Nazis and the Communists are the spiritual heirs of the Jacobin French Revolution and thereby servants of a political ideology which promises to transform the inner nature of man and wipe out all evil by revolutionary political and social processes. This infection is neither recent nor novel. It is a disposition of our existential selves; we are only precariously civilized, and "within us there is the propensity, persistent as the force of gravity, to revert under stress and strain, under neglect or temptation, to our first natures." [36]

The second realm of being is that of *essence.* It is a nonmaterial realm, and it has for Lippmann an almost exclusively rational character. It is that realm where objects are not materialized to the senses, but "where they are present to the mind." [37] In this realm

[34] Lippmann, "Man's Image of Man," *Commonweal,* XXXV (1942), 407.

[35] Cf. *The Public Philosophy,* 70.

[36] *Ibid.,* 71.

[37] *Ibid.,* 109.

one perceives the true and undistorted nature of things. It is a transcendent world in which man's souls can be regenerate and at peace. Within this recognizably Platonic region man's spirit, his essence, is at home.

Practical problems have their source in the fact that in earthly life man is necessarily involved primarily in existence, the first realm, rather than essence, the second. He cannot hope, therefore, to achieve perfection, and it is a confusing and disordering delusion if any man or social group believes such perfection possible. The ideals of existence must necessarily be worldly ideals, raising no expectation about the highest good. "They are concerned with the best that is possible among moral and finite, diverse and conflicting men." Because man's condition is one of flux and change, there can be no final conceptual definitions of such earthy ideals as liberty, equality, fraternity, and justice. "The different meanings are rather like different clothes, each good for a season, for certain weather, and for a time of day, none good for all times." [38]

Does this mean that there are no fixed points to which existential man can look for sure guidance? No, says Lippmann, for there is potentially available to him the realm of the spirit, "a realm of being in which the problems of earthly existence are not solved but transcended." The wisdom of this realm cannot be applied to the existential world in any casuistic fashion, since there is a hiatus between this highest wisdom and the actual perplexities with which men deal. The knowledge of essence is, however, intimately related to human conduct, for it affects the nature of man in that the essential vision of men transformed can and does modify their appetites and passions.

The twin concepts of two realms and two natures impinge upon what Lippmann sees revealed in the contemporary crisis as the central problem of man: the resolution of the inner conflict between the demands for freedom and for order. With the modern collapse of man's capacity to believe in "the invisible, the intangi-

[38] *Ibid.*, 110–11.

ble, and the imponderable," [39] he lost his essential anchors in objective criteria of right and truth. Existentially emancipated from authority, man has experienced in the most excruciating way the anguish into which the delusion of unlimited freedom can plunge the soul. Since the breakdown of public order which occurred during the First World War, multitudes have had no sense of security. Men find themselves unable to cope with the insoluble difficulties of unordered freedom. There exists a profound disorientation in their experience, "a radical disconnection between the notions of their minds and the needs of their souls." Such men have become Riesman's "lonely crowd," Durkheim's "anomic mass," Toynbee's "proletariat," of but not in the society where they live.[40]

If man is to recover his identity under these circumstances, he must first redefine freedom. Freedom properly understood is, for Lippmann, still the prime aim of existential man, but the actualization of freedom is set out in a new (yet very ancient) way: "We are free if we have the faculty of knowing what we *ought* to do and have the will to do it." [41]

Recognizing that man is caught up in the tension between the two realms and the matching conflict of his own two natures, Lippmann is no longer able to propose for society's political problems the simplistic solution of a rational elite who can interpret, inform, guide, and rule the irrational masses. What he has described is now recognized as a universal human predicament. Under these circumstances, his answer is to invoke anew the "traditions of civility"—the distilled wisdom of Western thought and historical experience—by which men are taught that the two realms are inseparable but disparate and that humanity must work

[39] *Ibid.*, 88.

[40] *Ibid.*, 86–87. Cf. David Riesman, *The Lonely Crowd* (New Haven, 1950); Emile Durkheim, *Suicide* (2 vols.; Glencoe, Ill., 1951); and Arnold Toynbee, *A Study of History* (12 vols., London, 1934–61). All are cited by Lippmann. Lippmann feels that man's predicament has been best described by Erich Fromm in *Escape from Freedom*. See *The Public Philosophy*, 87.

[41] *The Public Philosophy*, 111. The italics are in the original.

70

out its destiny in the balance between them. The two realms cannot be fused; neither can they be isolated or compartmentalized.
Life is lived in the interaction between them. Only as man recognizes and embraces this tension in the continuing quest to develop
internally the rule of the true self, the "civilized self," is he qualified either to rule or to be ruled.[42]

The validity and strength of this concept of man in Lippmann's
mature thought must undergo further investigation. Clearly, however, he believes that for men to be "good" men, their second
natures must exercise the power of life or death over their first or
fallen natures.

If he is correct, then only as the realm of essence masters the self-
centered, passionate realm of the first self can man fully participate
—as he is born to do—in the community of men, the good society. Only to the extent that society operates under the judgment
of the transcendent structures of order—structures which are
mirrored in the essence of man—does it become a good society.
Only in such a society are men no longer barbarians but truly
civilized. And only in such a society can civilization—shaped according to any rational definition of the term—long survive.

[42] See Lippmann, "On the Unity of Mankind," *Rotarian*, LXXI (October, 1947), 9: ". . . we may define a civilized man as one who is converted
to the belief that there are universal standards of law, of right, of justice,
which all men, when they are rational, are bound to acknowledge."

*How can this planet be governed by people who have
ceased to believe that there is good and there is evil,
that there are obligations that cannot be denied, who
insist, often with a show of learning, that what is
most convenient is right and what is most pleasing
to hear is true, or at least as true as anything can or
needs to be?*

WALTER LIPPMANN

Chapter III

The Maladies of Democracy

Political philosophy tends to fall generally into one of two categories: either it is primarily concerned with abstractions, or else it
is involved in and evolves from the concrete workings of the political process. Almost all of Walter Lippmann's numerous writings
are clearly *livres de circonstance*. His profession as a practicing
journalist has helped to prevent any tendency he might possibly
have had to stretch the elastic relationship between ideas and
events so far as to risk irrelevance. Never minted in a vacuum, his
political views have consistently borne the unmistakable stamp of
contemporary history.

The central peg on which Lippmann's thought hangs is his paramount evaluation of human personality. Consequently, he has
asked in varied ways and from diverse perspectives: what structure
of political organization most adequately meets the needs and pro-
tects the integrity of man as a person? No real doubt has ever existed
in Lippmann's judgment as to the general answer to that question. In the context of a modern, technological society he has
always been committed to some form of liberal democracy as the
best type of government for a nation like the United States.

Combined with his ability to assume a detached attitude and,

71

thereby, to see all sides of any question, Lippmann's analytical approach to politics has not allowed him to stop with a simple blanket endorsement of democracy. He has concerned himself with a constructive critique of the democratic system in operation, striving to lay bare its maladies and weaknesses. What specific elements within the comprehensive framework of American constitutional democracy, he has asked, most effectively fulfill the true purposes of government? No human organizational pattern is ever perfect, and only as those who support the Western concepts of freedom are honest in their self-criticism can the nation hope to maintain liberal democracy as a vital force in the modern world. Contrary to the accusations of some unfriendly observers, Lippmann has proved himself a valuable adherent of democracy in the act of fulfilling his role as an unabashed, intelligent critic of the political status quo.

To set out Lippmann's thought in this area, it will be helpful, first of all, to look at his specific indictment of one important technique used in the democratic process—that of majority rule. Following this consideration, it will be easier to understand his broader analysis of the roles of the people and of their leaders.

The Problem of Majority Rule

Obviously, no democracy, in any generally understood sense of the term, can function without reliance on the mechanism of decision-making through majority rule. Some authorities have gone so far as to classify rule by the majority as *the* distinguishing mark of democratic government. For instance, James Bryce has defined democracy as "government in which the will of the majority of qualified citizens rules." [1] Unwilling to venture quite so far, a contemporary theorist like Charles Frankel will affirm only that democracy prevents exclusive rule by any minority. [2] While it is true that most students of political theory would have numerous qualifications and explanations to append to any definition of

[1] James B. Bryce, *Modern Democracies* (New York, 1921), I, 26.
[2] Charles Frankel, *The Democratic Prospect* (New York, 1962), 42.

democracy in terms of majority rule, few, if any, would seek to eliminate it as one of several central facets.

To be stressed in the beginning is the fact, sometimes ignored by critics of Lippmann, that he has never advocated the elimination of majority rule as a practical democratic mechanism. He has been doubtful, for instance, of the value of such devices as proportional representation for all minority groups, since he recognizes the practical necessity of a working majority consensus in governmental decision. While vigorously attacking the elevation of any simple technique to the status of a democratic idol, Lippmann has also stated: "The rule of fifty-one per cent is a convenience, it is for certain matters a satisfactory political device, it is for others the lesser of two evils, and for still others, it is acceptable because we do not know any less troublesome method of obtaining a political decision. But it may easily become an absurd tyranny if we regard it worshipfully as though it were more than a political device." [3] The problem, as Lippmann sees it, lies not in the necessary use of the mechanism, but rather in the investing of a mere device with mystical significance and the power of determining truth and right.

Lippmann's first doubts about majority rule arose during his short stay in Schenectady as a city official in 1912. Mayor George Lunn, a Socialist, had been elected by a majority of the city's voters; yet, Lippmann soon learned, the vote of the majority carried with it no clear mandate for government policy. Actually, the majority had voted for a man, expressing confidence in his prospective leadership. Most of the voters were not Socialists and knew little about the intricacies of Socialism. In no reasonable way could it be argued that their votes as such put any stamp of truth or rightness upon the actual policies of a Socialist administration. Lippmann declared in A Preface to Politics that voting is a statistical method, "neither so conclusive as the devotees say, nor so bad as the people who are awed by it would like to believe." At that time, consistent with his conviction that the proper func-

[3] Lippmann, "Why Should the Majority Rule?" Harpers, CLII (1926), 404.

tion of government was to fulfill the instinctive though inarticulate needs of the people, he argued that the value of voting was not that it extracted wisdom from the multitudes in some unexplainable fashion, but that it furnished wisdom about the people. Lippmann approved majority rule on the purely pragmatic basis that an election showed "the quantitative division of the people on several alternatives. That choice is not necessarily wise, but it is wise to heed that choice." [4]

From the beginning, therefore, Lippmann had few illusions about the caliber of wisdom arising from the action of the majority. In 1913 his view of human nature and its impulses led him to put a value on majority rule which he would not later sustain: the idea that it did in some way help translate the desires and needs of the people as a whole into understandable form. At the same time, he even then considered rule by the majority simply one of many democratic devices. And he was concerned that the voices of minorities not be stifled, as they might be if the decisions of the majority were accepted as the voice of God. Only as minorities were fully heard and their views in some sense heeded was the cause of truth rightly served. This emphasis on the role of the minority in a free government led him to expand and clarify his own definition of democracy. Mere majority rule could not be taken as the distinguishing mark. Even if the majority was actually unanimous, the sytem was still not automatically democratic. "Democracy is a meaningless word unless it signifies that differences of opinion have been expressed, represented, and even satisfied in the decision." [5]

By the time Lippmann had passed through the years of World War I, observed the power of propaganda on men's minds, and studied the practical effects of twisted and biased news coverage and interpretation, he was ready to launch more specific attacks on the overestimation of the meaning of majority rule.

In 1922 he threw down the gauntlet to those who held Rousseau-like beliefs in the character of majority rule as expressive of

[4] A Preface to Politics, 115.
[5] The Stakes of Diplomacy (New York, 1915), 111.

the true general will. These ideas he characterized as constituting a democratic mythology. "It is quite easy to become mystical on the subject. You can say that out of the vasty deeps of our modern minds, out of the eternal caverns of the unconscious, out of the collective super-soul and over-soul, profounder than reason, impregnated with the everlasting memories of the race, instinctive with primal knowledge and heavy laden with immemorial wisdom, comes the will of the people. . . ." [6]

For Lippmann, such concepts were meaningless. In *Public Opinion* he assaulted the faith of the early eighteenth century democrats who relied on a spontaneous welling up of "reasoned righteousness" out of the masses of men. "All of them hoped that it would, many of them believed that it did, although the cleverest, like Thomas Jefferson, had all sorts of private reservations." [7] With belief in the traditional authorities of the church, the Bible, and God-given leaders shaken, popular sovereignty had become the touchstone of democracy, providing an answer to the need for an infallible origin for the new social order. Arguing against the entrenched power of royalty, aristocracy, wealth, and heirarchy, the advocates of people's government were almost forced to maintain the empirically untenable doctrine of mystic wisdom in the popular will—a will expressed through majority rule. But, argued Lippmann, modern knowledge and experience are incontrovertible in their demonstration that the manipulation of popular consent and the creation of necessary majorities on election day are techniques. "Within the life of this generation now in control of affairs, persuasion has become a self-conscious art and a regular organ of popular government . . . it is no daring prophecy to say that the knowledge of how to create consent will alter every political calculation and modify every political premise." [8]

His study of the workings of public opinion led Lippmann to foresee the giant propaganda machines devised in the middle

[6] Lippmann, "Second-Hand Statesmen," *Yale Review*, n.s. XI (1922), 681.
[7] *Public Opinion*, 257.
[8] *Ibid.*, 248.

twentieth century, both for such a relatively harmless end as the increase of toothpaste sales and for the demonic design of remaking human personality completely in the totalitarian mold. In the face of such prospects, majority rule lost more and more of its credentials as a dependable guide to truth and reasonable policy.

The idolizing of majority rule appeared to Lippmann to have come about as the result of a misinterpretation of the transfer of sovereignty. The attributes assigned to kings under a theory of divine right had been assigned in popular democratic theory to the people, acting through a majority. "Yet the inherent absurdity of making vision and wisdom dependent on fifty-one per cent of any collection of men has always been apparent." Even a divinely appointed ruler had always been conceived as subject to the limits of a higher law, and Lippmann saw the entire complicated code of protection for the civil rights of minorities as a practical recognition of the need for such limits in democracy as well. The justification for majority rule in politics was not to be found in a supposed ethical superiority; instead, it rested on the sheer necessity for finding a place in civilized society for the force residing in the weight of numbers. A ballot is "a civilized substitute for a bullet." [9]

Lippmann's most extreme views concerning majority rule were expressed in an article written in 1926. The year before, a young teacher named John Scopes had been tried at Dayton, Tennessee, for teaching the principles of evolution in violation of a state law. Using the Scopes trial as his test case, Lippmann contended that, in the light of the argument that unlimited majority rule is the accurate expression of the will of the people, William Jennings Bryan's position in the Scopes case was logically irrefutable: ". . . if the doctrine of majority rule is based on the eternal and inherent rights of man, then it is the only true basis for government, and there can be no fair objections to the moral basis of a law made by a fundamentalist majority in Tennessee." What was needed, said Lippmann, was a retreat from the doctrine held "carelessly but almost universally" in every Western democracy— the assumption that the majority must always rule. The Tennessee

[9] *The Phantom Public,* 58–59.

case, in which the fundamental tenet of popular government had been used to destroy that on which the whole hope of democracy rested—faith in popular education—demonstrated beyond doubt "that the dogma of majority rule contains within it some sort of deep and destructive confusion." [10]

Lippmann's analysis of this confusion was remarkable, particularly because it included early premonitions of a viewpoint—the concept of the two realms—which only matured years later. As the basic source of the misconception of majority rule, he posited a confusion between two levels of understanding. First, on the level of "primitive intuition," each man is convinced that, in some ultimate way, all men possess a fundamental equality. This insight is not scientifically demonstrable, but it possesses an "essential quality of feeling" which "is the same from Buddha to St. Francis to Whitman." Second, on the level of worldly reality, one must recognize the obvious, experimentally verifiable differences among men in terms of talent, training, and ability. In the course of history, men have seized upon the first of these philosophies and applied it, recklessly and often without justification, to the realm of actual life. "Thus the doctrine that I am as good as you in eternity because all the standards of goodness are finite and temporary was converted into the doctrine that I am as good as you are in this world by this world's standards." When the implications of this confusion had been fully developed, it meant that no distinctions of value could be made; one man's notion or idea was as good as another's. "If I feel strongly about it, it is right; there is no other test." No objective method remained by which to decide the relative value of opinions.

In this situation there is no way, in a democracy, to choose between opinions except to count them, Lippmann said. The mystical sense of equality is translated to mean that two minds are superior to one mind and two souls better than one soul. Majority rule becomes the only practical avenue of arriving at whatever is

[10] "Why Should the Majority Rule?" 400. This paragraph and the following three paragraphs contain a summary of this important article, and all quotations are taken from it.

to pass for truth. What this finally means is that the dogma of majority rule, under modern conditions, is not, after all, based on a specious claim to some magical access to greater wisdom or virtue, but upon the fact that the final practical determinant of "truth" is force. Normally, the greater number possesses the greater force.

At Dayton Mr. Bryan contended that in schools supported by the state the majority of the voters had a right to determine what should be taught. If my analysis is correct, there is no fact from which that right can be derived except the fact that the majority is stronger than the minority. It cannot be argued that the majority in Tennessee represented the whole people of Tennessee; nor that fifty-one Tennesseeans are better than forty-nine Tennesseeans; nor that they were better biologists, or better Christians, or better parents, or better Americans. It cannot be said they are necessarily more in tune with the ultimate judgments of God. All that can be said for them is that there are more of them, and that in a world ruled for force it may be necessary to defer to the force they exercise.[11]

Such an interpretation presented a grim picture, though Lippmann lightened it a bit in the concluding paragraphs of his article. If majority rule is simply another name for rule by superior power, then the minority must yield to it, but in a democracy they need not accept the result as final. When the true meaning of majority rule is untangled from the accretions that have given it false unction, the hope is that the dissident factions in a democracy will feel more free to voice their objections and to employ persuasion of all types to turn their minority into a majority. This, for Lippmann, constitutes the central core of democratic functioning. But its efficacy is limited so long as the superstition of sanctity surrounding majority rule has not been exorcised.

Corresponding to the expansion of Lippmann's understanding of majority rule was a change of attitude toward the work of the Founding Fathers in devising the American Constitution. In *A Preface to Politics,* written while Lippmann was still suspicious of

[11] Probably, Lippmann misunderstood Bryan. Bryan's ultimate source of authority was not actually the will of the majority but the literal interpretation of the Bible. It is almost certain that Bryan would have opposed the teaching of evolution (since he believed it contradicted Scripture) even had the majority supported such teaching.

anything which did not allow the basic impulses of human nature a maximum of constructive expression, he was highly critical of the Constitution, calling it "the most important instance we have of the deliberate application of a mechanical philosophy in human affairs." He referred disdainfully to "the fantastic attempts to circumvent human folly by balancing it with vetoes and checks." [12] His later reflections convinced him, however, that the authors of the Constitution used more wisdom than he had given them credit for. Aware of the dangers involved in the unrestricted rule of "transient majorities," they set up checks and balances "which would, as they put it, 'refine the will' of the people." [13] The Constitution, Lippmann asserted, does not really prevent the people from doing what they want to do; what it does is to make it impossible for a temporary majority to do that about which they have had little or no time to think. The constitutional concern was that the nation might be certain that "Philip sober and not Philip drunk" would do the legislating.[14]

Lippmann's 1926 article in *Harper's* had expressed the low point in his estimate of majority rule. During the decade and a half between 1926 and the beginning of World War II, his attitude underwent an interesting dual development. On the positive side, he became gradually more willing to soften his denunciations of the device and to admit for it some limited value as a method of arriving at "right" decisions. His cautious advance was in the direction of the ancient Aristotelian argument that, in a situation where free discussion and intelligent debate prevail, the majority is generally more *likely* to be right than the minority, though there is no guarantee.[15] On the other hand, Lippmann's worst fears of the consequences of unchecked majority rule were more than justified by events in Europe, especially in Germany. He watched elected representatives vote away the people's rights and then saw

[12] *A Preface to Politics*, 14.
[13] *The Method of Freedom* (New York, 1934), 74–75.
[14] Lippmann, "Challenge to the Constitution," *American Magazine*, CXIX (June, 1935), 99.
[15] See Lippmann, "The Indispensable Opposition," *Atlantic Monthly*, CLXIV (August, 1939), 186–90.

their actions endorsed in plebiscites by an overwhelming majority of the populace. "We have, in short, seen democracy commit suicide by majority vote." [16] Here was the actualizing of the disastrous possibilities inherent in defining democracy as the rule of the greater number. Even in his 1926 assessment, Lippmann had been arguing, at least implicitly, that majority rule is a dependable device only if it operates within certain limitations. What the limitations are, he could not then see with any assurance though he seemed to believe that some restrictions of function and qualification should apply; i.e., that qualified educators should operate schools, qualified scientists carry on scientific investigations, etc., free from interference by unqualified majorities. In the light of the events of the 1930's, his recognition of the inadequacy of this argument set Lippmann searching for more viable and effective limits.

Still, as late as 1938, long after the results of the tragic debacle of German liberalism had become clear, Lippmann was willing to rest his hopes for a restrained democracy on a set of mechanisms— the delaying devices of a constitutional government of checks and balances. Admitting that there was no final guarantee in the Constitution of the basic liberties of speech, press, and conscience, since a sizable majority of voters might eventually repeal the Bill of Rights, he contended that the American democracy was so strongly entrenched and so well organized as to make a totalitarian dictatorship unthinkable. "No frame of government can absolutely guarantee human liberty," he said. "But the American system, whatever its other faults may be, is the most ingeniously and elaborately contrived mechanism on earth to make it difficult to abolish liberty in a gust of popular passion." [17] It was to require the full impact of World War II and its aftermath to convince Lippmann that even the cleverest governmental mechanism was susceptible to corruption, once the underlying philosophic structure sustaining and justifying it had disappeared.

Among students of political theory, Lippmann's overall ap-

[16] Lippmann, address at William and Mary College on April 23, 1937, reported in New York *Herald-Tribune*, April 24, 1937, 34.
[17] "Today and Tomorrow," February 1, 1938.

praisal of majority rule has been much discussed and criticized. It has been pointed out—and rightly so—that he has overemphasized the concept of majority rule as a pure expression of force.[18] The efficacy of majority rule does not rest wholly upon the threat of force by the more numerous power group, though it is true that such a threat can always be understood as potentially existent. But force rests finally on authority, and in a democracy authority is always a function of active consent and voluntary will. In a working democracy minorities abide by majority decisions, not simply because they are afraid of the consequences otherwise, but because they are committed to a community of consent, in which it is normally conceived to be proper and right either to obey the law, or, if one disagrees strongly, to test its validity through legal processes. Of course, it is clear from later writings like *The Public Philosophy* that Lippmann also recognizes this element as central in democracy; yet, much of his analysis of majority rule has given the impression that he ignored a vital facet, perhaps in his desire to emphasize the eventual perils of an unchecked rule of the transient majority.

It can also be pointed out, in rebuttal to some of Lippmann's more extreme denunciations, that the practical alternative to majority rule is always minority rule. In later years Lippmann seems to have given more credence to this argument, and he has devoted himself more and more to unraveling the intricate problem of how to restrain the rule of a majority while, at the same time, preventing the exercise of undue power by some minority group. His efforts in this direction, as we have seen, led him first to rely upon procedural practices. In the final analysis the majority must make the decisions if the governing process is to be carried out successfully, but the majority in a truly liberal democracy *must rule in a certain way*. So long as majority determinations of policy are open decisions, arrived at after free discussion and subject to continuing debate and possible amendment, the danger of tyranny is alleviated. Thus, commitment by any people to democracy involves

[18] See David Spitz, *Patterns of Anti-Democratic Thought* (New York, 1949), 86–87.

also a necessary commitment to the nondebatable and nonalterable core of free procedures which make democracy possible. It was on this kind of reasoning that the final arguments of *The Good Society* rested. The more profound question of the philosophical, or even theological, presuppositions on which the commitment to democracy may ultimately be based, Lippmann left materially unanswered until the writing of *The Public Philosophy*.

The People and the Elite

Underlying all of Lippmann's discussion of the issue of majority rule is a deeper and more complex query: in a democracy, what role are the people actually competent to play? Much of the material which enters into his answer to this question, as it developed across the years, has been introduced in the preceding chapter. Lippmann's estimate of the proper role of the people in government is naturally linked with his basic understanding of human nature. What kind of people we are determines what part we are qualified to assume in politics.

For instance, when one goes back to 1913 and 1914, one is immediately struck with the uncertainty of Lippmann's attitude toward the people as a whole. He himself identified this ambivalence as one of the continuing paradoxes of the democratic movement: ". . . it loves a crowd and fears the individuals who compose it." [19] The difficulty arose out of, on the one hand, an idealistic commitment to government by the uninhibited consent of the governed, and, on the other, an empirical recognition of the inability of most men adequately to carry out their complex political responsibilities. Historically, Lippmann thought, democratic theorists had attempted to resolve this difficulty by installing mechanical contrivances, such as a system of checks and balances, designed to permit the people to govern and yet, also, to restrain them from extremes. As has been pointed out, Lippmann later came to support essentially the same position, but in 1913 he

[19] *A Preface to Politics*, 17.

emphatically rejected such artificial devices as incompatible with a realistic politics of human nature.

The alternative suggested by the early Lippmann has been outlined. A dual approach, it carried with it the baggage of his ambivalent attitude toward the people. Lippmann had argued that democracy must necessarily trust instinctive, irrational human desires to point to ends which provide both individual happiness and social harmony. In his thought, however, strict limits were imposed on the extent of the confidence which can be placed in the masses. Instinctively, human beings want the right things, but they do not usually know the best ways in which to satisfy their desires. Hemmed in by a society which is not adapted to the constructive fulfillment of these basic human needs, men are forced to express their impulses in ways which are personally debilitating and socially upsetting. To offset this situation, Lippmann introduced the concept of an elite, the "innovator," a type of natural leader best described as one who regards government as a problem to be solved, rather than as a routine to be administered. A creative, intuitive leader, in touch with the pulse of the people and aware of their needs, can marshal social engineers and experts to provide more effective and significant avenues of expression.

From the first, even during his most optimistic moments, Lippmann has always located the prime problem of democracy in the same place: the competence of the masses to govern. He has not questioned their right to do so; rather, he has sought to deal realistically with the ramifications of this right in the light of modern society's complexities. As far back as 1909, as a college student, Lippmann wrote, "If the people are to rule, they must be an active, jealous people. Unless the average man today is able to feel as the Greeks are said to have felt, that the state is the 'expression of the highest and best nature of the citizen'; . . . democracy must by the nature of things become honeycombed with corruption." [20] He was even more specific in 1914: ". . . we have to face the fact in America that what thwarts the growth of our civilization is not

[20] "Harvard in Politics: A Problem in Imperceptibles," 97.

the uncanny, malicious contrivance of the plutocracy, but the faltering method, the distracted soul, and the murky vision of what we call grandiloquently the will of the people." [21]

For this knotty difficulty Lippmann's prescriptions have generally been consistent. In one way or another, and with varying hopes of success, he has advocated, first of all, a continuing educational attempt to lift the level of men's competence to act as free citizens. This has been his long-run remedy for democracy's maladies. In the interim, his immediate suggestion has been that democracy cannot survive long enough for its citizenry to be educated adequately without the exercise of strong leadership by a democratic elite.

To trace the outlines of his thought concerning the function of education is revealing, for a graph of this development would match a charting of Lippmann's optimism and pessimism about human nature. His estimate of the effectiveness and content of the education best adapted to the strengthening of democracy has been modified considerably by the passage of time. In 1913 Lippmann was highly critical of the then prevailing educational methods and curriculum. Based on what he considered the old-fashioned idea that mankind should be "harnessed to" abstract principles —liberty, justice, equality, such education succeeded largely only in bringing about a "natural ossification of mind," thoroughly hostile to invention and innovation.[22] By contrast, what was required was training in the scientific method, the psychology of human nature, and the pragmatic use of reason, so that men might efficiently organize society for the achieving of human needs and desires.

By the time *Drift and Mastery* was written, Lippmann had become even more certain of the necessity for widespread scientific training as the bulwark of democracy. "Democracy in politics is the twin brother of scientific thinking," he said. Science is "the unfrightened, masterful, and humble approach to reality—the needs

[21] *Drift and Mastery*, xvi.
[22] *A Preface to Politics*, 29, 84.

of our natures and the possibilities of the world." [23] In proportion to the spread of scientific discipline, society's problems can be met and mastered.

In the next few years, however, Lippmann came to have serious doubts as to the practical scope of education. The obvious difficulties which the average man experiences in attempting to obtain an understanding of complex political situations caused Lippmann to rethink the efficacy of the educational process. He did not doubt the basic capacity of all men for learning. "There is, then," he wrote in 1923, "no slightest reason for losing faith in the one human activity [education] which amidst all the bewilderment of these times gives the most certain promise of a better world." [24] The problem lies in man's loss of contact with objective information. In a highly technical society facts, knowledge, interpretation —all had become second hand to most men. "And a society which lives at second-hand will commit incredible follies and countenance inconceivable brutalities if that contact is intermittent and untrustworthy. . . ." [25]

By 1925 Lippmann had reached the nadir of his pessimism concerning the practical results of mass education. The source of his pessimism was not exclusively a low evaluation of the average man's ability; more directly, it stemmed from an increased perception of the almost incredible complexity of society. "The private citizen today," he wrote, "has come to feel rather like a deaf spectator in the back row, who ought to keep his mind on the mystery off there, but cannot quite manage to keep awake." [26] The problems of a complicated, industrialized environment appeared to change more rapidly than even the teachers could grasp them, and certainly much faster than they could convey their meaning to a population of children. The hope which remained was that education, instead of majoring on facts and information, might

[23] *Drift and Mastery,* 275.
[24] Lippmann, "In Defense of Education," *The Century,* CVI (May, 1923), 103.
[25] "The Basic Problem of Democracy," 625.
[26] *The Phantom Public,* 13.

be able to instill a pattern of thought which would permit the citizen to approach new problems in some minimally effective manner. The shift of emphasis was from the imparting of undistorted facts to the teaching of a basic philosophic attitude toward problems. Such a shift was prophetic of the major thesis of A *Preface to Morals*: that the secret of human maturity is the development of a disinterested attitude toward life's circumstances.

Lippmann's changing perspective on education paralleled his changing conception of the public's role in political processes. Never had he argued in favor of the myth of the omnicompetent citizen; always he had postulated the need for a specially gifted governing class. But his estimate of the people's competence was drastically modified as he became more conscious of the difficulties involved in educating men accurately to define and judge political issues. In 1919 he had asserted that the distortion of news was democracy's major problem, a judgment that carried with it the corollary that, given adequate access to the facts, most men could exercise reasonable effectiveness in the governing process.[27] By the middle twenties, however, his research in the field of public opinion had altered that conviction. He came to feel that, badly needed as objective, impartial information agencies are, they alone are not sufficient to enable intelligent participation in policy-making and administration. Men can elect their major officials, express approval or disapproval in general terms of overall policy, and insist that government avail itself of the resources of fact-finding agencies; but this is the limit of the public's effective role. The actual business of government must be carried out by the experts. Indeed, in an extreme mood of pessimism, which corresponded to his most discouraged views of education's possibilities, Lippmann argued in *The Phantom Public* that the best the people could hope to do was to elect those men to office who showed a willingness to abide by accepted procedural rules; that is, to act reasonably, deliberately, and without arbitrary judgment.

[27] See Lippmann, "Unrest," *New Republic*, XX (1919), 322: ". . . my own hopes are in what might be called the latent public. . . . Intolerance may submerge them for a time and timidity paralyze them and conformity subdue them. They are there. They can be summoned."

The full extent of Lippmann's limitations upon the public, as proposed at this state of his thought, can only be realized by a study of his suggested guidelines for public action:

1. Executive action is not for the public. The public acts only by aligning itself as the partisan of some one in a position to act executively.
2. The intrinsic merits of a question are not for the public.
3. The anticipation, the analysis, and the solution of a question are not for the public.
4. The specific, technical, intimate criteria required in the handling of a question are not for the public. The public's criteria are generalized for many problems; they turn essentially on procedure . . . .
5. What is left for the public is a judgment as to whether the actors in a controversy are following a settled rule of behavior or their own arbitrary desires.
6. . . . it is necessary to discover criteria, suitable to the nature of public opinion, which can be relied on to distinguish between reasonable and arbitrary behavior.
7. For the purposes of social action, reasonable behavior is conduct which follows a settled course whether in making a rule, in enforcing it, or in amending it.[28]

The radical nature of Lippmann's indictment of public competence was itself the thing which rendered his suggested rules inherently impractical. If the people were actually as spasmodic, superficial, and defective in their political knowledge as Lippmann pictured them, how could they possibly be expected to exercise the tremendous amount of political restraint called for by his program? As a reviewer of his book expressed it: "Now the plain facts are that the public . . . is marked by active sentiments and conceptions about right and wrong, the desirable and the undesirable, and that part of its essence is to opinionate about politics, projects, and panaceas." [29] That any real change in the state of affairs could be achieved by simply exhorting the public to cease meddling in matters which did not concern it was a flimsy hope.

It has been shown that Lippmann's confidence in the public

[28] *The Phantom Public*, 144–45.
[29] Harold D. Lasswell, review of *The Phantom Public*, in *American Journal of Sociology*, XXXI (1926), 535.

capacity to govern, along with his trust in education, was at its highest, most optimistic level in the early, pre-war stages of his thought. After World War I, it steadily descended. When he wrote *The Phantom Public* in 1925, he put into words his most pessimistic views of the people's role and, indeed, virtually ruled the masses out of anything but an occasional, somewhat traumatic intervention in the political process. It was, perhaps, inevitable that the pendulum should swing back from this extreme position.

A *Preface to Morals*, written four years later, represented some degree of reversal in attitude concerning both education and the public. Lippmann was once again hopeful of the eventual results of the right kind of teaching, since he now saw the indwelling tendencies of a technological society as propelling men toward scientific detachment and disinterest. In business, industry, morals, and government he observed this force at work, and he expected it to make its power felt increasingly through the educational system. Education should center its attention, he felt, upon the achievement of genuine maturity by pupils. "The problems of education are at bottom problems in how to lead the child from one stage of development to another until at last he becomes a harmonious and autonomous personality; . . ." [30] Scientific studies, producing the necessary objective viewpoint, should be seasoned with a healthy dose of aesthetics so as to cultivate an appreciation of harmony and symmetry as well as the refined and civilized expressions of the human spirit. Along with his more cheerful view of what education could do, Lippmann also raised his sights as to the eventual political role of the masses. He saw a measure of disinterestedness as within the reach of all men. In a society whose structure directs men toward such a maturity of outlook, there is the probability that more and more people will become capable of intelligent participation in political life.

The government in which disinterested men can take part, however, is of a particular type; and in this connection Lippmann faced a peculiar problem. His "politics of disinterest" led him to the conviction that the function of government is to provide and in-

[30] *A Preface to Morals*, 175.

sure as much genuine liberty as possible, in order that the mature, autonomous individual might attain his greatest personal potential. Government cannot plan or collectivize men's lives; this would be to violate their basic freedom. The political structure must operate, Lippmann thought, so as to preserve and guarantee wide areas of free and independent action for every man.

Such a philosophy impelled Lippmann, as we have seen, to oppose the Roosevelt New Deal, along with other manifestations of what he classed as collectivism. But a disturbing reality remained to be dealt with. Clearly, most men are not yet mature and disinterested, even though society is pushing in that direction. Immature men seek to infringe on other men's rights and must therefore be restrained by law. It is the government's task to do this restraining, under the direction, of course, of an elite of disinterested leaders. In *The Good Society* (1937), Lippmann set out his "agenda of liberalism," [31] a listing of the areas of action for a truly liberal government in insuring individual freedom. Actually, however, it is doubtful whether he proposed less government, or more. In practice, if not in theory, it is difficult to determine where Lippmann's brand of liberal democracy stopped and collectivism began—except in one respect, which he himself considered immensely important. In "the good society," all governmental action is ideally nonarbitrary, operating on men as persons and never as things, functioning under the restrictions of the humane Western tradition of common law.

In effect, the role outlined for the public in *The Good Society* was greatly expanded beyond anything Lippmann had previously proposed, at least since his earliest days. The people were conceived to be the guardians of freedom, exercising their power through a government whose leaders are intelligently selected in accordance with a willingness to abide by the great constitutional tradition of the Western world. Since it was supposed that the job of the government would not be to regulate the lives of its citizens but to provide the necessary opportunities by which men could regulate their own lives, it was also assumed that men possess the

[31] *The Good Society*, 203–40.

initiative and ability to avail themselves of these opportunities. *The Good Society* was, in one sense, a renewed affirmation of faith in the capacity of most men to govern themselves; but it was a limited affirmation in that it applied finally only to those men who understand and accept the predominant traditions of Western culture. The affirmation was further guarded by the lingering thought in Lippmann's mind that those who actually administer the government and hold major places of responsibilities will be the mature, disinterested men depicted in *A Preface to Morals*. Thus, while he magnified the role of the public, he at the same time multiplied the responsibilities of the elite. His hope was, however, that the elite would gradually expand its numbers.

With the development of the thesis that government must be externally limited by the common law tradition, there followed a corresponding change in Lippmann's conception of the content of education. His new ideas, clearly set out in an article written in 1939, represented a drastic inversion of the content and values which had been essential in his pre-World War I theory. Where he had once scoffed at the slavery to tradition involved in any emphasis on abiding or self-evident truths, he now wrote:

The failure to teach an appreciation of the obvious and simple truths, what the authors of the Declaration of Independence would have called the self-evident truths, may not prevent the schools from turning out clever men, well-informed men, even learned men. But it will prevent them from turning out wise men. For what distinguishes a wise man from a man who has merely acquired knowledge is that the wise man possesses a fund of elementary and self-evident principles by which he can test the reports he receives, the theories that are advanced, by which he can decide whether or not the knowledge that is offered to him violates the conclusions of human experience.[32]

Lippmann thus reached the conclusion that neither the teaching of raw facts, nor the inculcation of detachment by the scientific method, nor the increase of aesthetic appreciation can, in isolation,

[32] Lippmann, "National Defense Through Patriotic Education," *National Defense News*, III (April–May, 1939), 9.

insure and guarantee that any man will be committed to the fundamentals of democracy or capable of good citizenship. More is required, and Lippmann found what he felt is needed by turning to the accumulated wisdom and experience of the past as a firm basis for thought and action in the present. "All the great educators, beginning with Plato and Aristotle, have insisted that training in the art of distinguishing good and evil must precede the making of practical judgments in human affairs." [33] Unless the mainstream of Western culture, with its insistence on human values and objective standards of right and wrong, can be restored to the educational curriculum, Lippmann sees the years ahead as belonging to "tyrants, demagogues, and mediocrities." [34]

One special phase of the democratic heritage which Lippmann now sees as essential is pertinent at this point. He has concluded that any discussion of the role of the people in government is misleading unless there is first a clear definition of the term, "the people." For himself, he has gone for an appropriate definition to the thought of Edmund Burke, who was not willing simply to identify "The People," in its broad sense, with the body of voters at any one time. "The People" represent the "entire living population, with their predecessors and successors." As Lippmann employs the concept, it stands for the corporate nation, the continuous and connected generations, of whom Burke spoke when he invoked the partnership "not only between those who are living" but also with "those who are dead, and those who are to be born." "The People" is an entity whose constituents come and go, but the entity endures. Obviously, from this perspective, no plurality of voters, ex-

[33] "Today and Tomorrow," July 4, 1942.

[34] *Ibid.* For a concise statement of Lippmann's position on education, see his address, "State of Education in this Troubled Age," *Vital Speeches,* VII (1941), 200–203. He stated his thesis as follows: "That during the past forty or fifty years those who are responsible for education have progressively removed from the curriculum of studies the Western culture which produced the modern democratic state; . . . That our civilization cannot effectively be maintained where it still flourishes, or be restored where it has been crushed, without the revival of the central, continuous, and perennial culture of the Western world. . . ."

pressing their preference at any one time, can determine the will of "The People." "In fact, demogoguery can be described as the sleight of hand by which a fraction of The People as voters are invested with the authority of *The People*. That is why so many crimes are committed in the people's name." [35]

This definition is, of course, open to attack as abstract and in a practical sense as meaningless. Lippmann takes note of this line of argument by citing "that resolute nominalist, Jeremy Bentham," who contended that "the community is a fictitious body, composed of the individual persons who are considered as constituting as it were its *members*. The interest of the community then is, what?—The sum of the interests of the several members who compose it." [36] But Bentham's seemingly empirical and matter-of-fact approach is not without weaknesses of its own. As Lippmann observes, "the several members who compose" the community are never the same from hour to hour. Some die; some are born. The community is constantly in the flux of historical continuity. Like it or not, it is inextricably involved in history, both past and future.

But, Lippmann's critics have said, even if this be true, what practical good is the concept? How can one possibly know the political sentiments of "cadavers and unknown spirits"? [37] It was to answer this kind of question that Lippmann moved into an investigation of what he calls "the public philosophy." The public philosophy constitutes, in one sense, the accumulated wisdom of "The People," tested and tried by experience. In another sense, it is far more than this, for it embodies a particular pattern of values, as well as basic presuppositions about man and his world, which men have not invented. Instead, argues Lippmann, the core of the public philosophy is *found* in the nature of man and existence and is thereby entitled to be referred to as *natural law*. Only a body of citizens, including both the governing and the governed, who have

[35] *The Public Philosophy*, 32, 35, 34.
[36] *Ibid.*, 34.
[37] Charles B. Forcey, "Leadership and 'Misrule by the People,'" *New Republic*, CXXXII (1955), 14.

been educated in the context and the content of this public philosophy can provide the necessary dynamic for the successful operation of liberal democracy.

Without such education, without such a public philosophy—alive and functioning—Lippmann argues that democracy suffers from a chronic illness, one which may indeed prove to be terminal in nature.

*"Human life," says Whitehead, "is driven forward
by its dim apprehension of notions too general for
existing language." The dim apprehension that
there must be a law higher than the arbitrary will of
any man has driven civilized men forward seeking to
tame the barbarian that is in us all, and by usages,
laws, and institutions to achieve what Plato called
the victory of persuasion over force.*

WALTER LIPPMANN

Chapter IV

The Meaning and Function
of Law

If, as Lippmann maintains, the main preoccupation of Western
political thought for at least two thousand years has been the attempt to find a law superior to arbitrary power,[1] any analysis of
political philosophy is required to pay due attention to the philosopher's understanding of law's meaning and function.

Few questions concerning human society have been asked so
persistently and answered in such diverse ways as the question
"What is law?" Even a cursory glance at the various approaches to
the problem indicates the extent of the difficulty involved. While
almost anyone can confidently cite examples of law if he is asked
to do so, the problem of a general definition setting out salient
characteristics which will identify all laws continues to be a puzzling one. Is a law valid—is it actually law at all—if it is not, or
cannot be, enforced? What about statutory enactments, such as
some of the German Nazi legislation, which flagrantly violate generally accepted codes of morality and justice? Are these acts to be

[1] *The Good Society,* 5.

considered law on the same level as other statutes, or do they contravene some "higher law"? How do laws differ from simple social rules? Such queries only begin to uncover the perplexities of the problem.

The attempt to find a formula for expressing the distinctive essence of law has produced many definitions, some of which sound decidedly unreal and artificial to the uninitiated. The law is "what officials do about disputes . . ."—so goes one statement.[2] Or, in the provocative words of Lippmann's old friend, Justice Holmes: "The prophecies of what the courts will do . . . are what I mean by law."[3] Law expresses the "common conviction" of a community concerning what is just, contends another authority.[4] "Not so," replies Hans Kelsen. "Law is the stipulation of a sanction,"[5] or in other words, the statement of the punishment or consequence provided for any particular action or failure to act. Other legal theorists have sought the essence of law in custom, in the dictates of reason, in the undisputed command of a sovereign, or in religious revelation. No one approach has been fully satisfactory nor has any achieved universal acceptance. The pattern of Walter Lippmann's understanding of the nature of law must be viewed against the background of this kind of general uncertainty.

What Is Law?

In one of the clearest and most helpful recent treatments of the subject of law, H. L. A. Hart has suggested that three recurrent issues create most of the speculation about the nature of legal acts: "How does law differ from and how is it related to orders backed by threat? How does legal obligation differ from, and how is it related to, moral obligation? What are rules and to what ex-

[2] Karl N. Llewellyn, *The Bramble Bush* (New York, 1951), 9.
[3] Oliver Wendell Holmes, "The Path of the Law," *Collected Papers* (New York, 1920), 173.
[4] Cf. Ernest Barker, *Principles of Social and Political Theory* (Oxford, 1951).
[5] Hans Kelsen, *General Theory of Law and State* (Cambridge, Mass., 1945), 61.

tent is law an affair of rules?" [6] These questions introduce factors which figure prominently in most analyses of the meaning and function of law: coercion, morality, and procedural norms. Each legal philosopher usually tends to come down heavily on one of the three.

In the tracing of Walter Lippmann's thought, all three elements must play their part. Beginning with a viewpoint which stressed the true nature of law as its congeniality with basic patterns of irrational human nature, he soon modified his approach through a decisive stress on the role of coercion. In the course of his argument supporting this stance, he found it expedient to introduce procedural validity as a norm, and soon he elevated this to make it the central legal theme. In the more recent expositions of his political theory, he has brought the moral aspect of law into prominence.

Lippmann's earliest political writings reveal a certain superficiality in his understanding of law. His interest prior to World War I was in the dynamic phases of democratic life—the power of energetic, pioneering leadership and the fluid adaptation of all political structure to the vast economic and psychological changes taking place in society. Freedom, not order, was his prime concern. Against the dynamic elements he ranged what he classed as mechanical forms, and included among these rigidities, seen principally as tools of nonprogressive order, was the contemporary interpretation of law, limiting and hampering man's mastery of his environment.

Lippmann described the traditional American legal attitude as one which conceived of government as operating within a "frame." The notion of the Constitution as a fundamental document, setting out once and for all the skeleton of government and its powers, was repugnant to him. In fact, he charged, "Only by violating the very spirit of the Constitution have we been able to preserve the letter of it." Most traditional conceptions of government by law impressed him as static theories, violating drastically his understanding of politics with human nature at its center. Thus, be-

[6] H. L. A. Hart, *The Concept of Law* (Oxford, 1961), 13.

hind the facade of law, he saw an "invisible government," "an empire of natural groups about natural leaders," [7] existing because it corresponds, in a way fossilized legal structures can never do, to the true nature of political power. This invisible pattern is actually far more important than the obvious and formal legal organization.

In A *Preface to Politics* Lippmann specifically attacked the standard conceptions of law's meaning, using a "Report on Social Evil" (issued by the Chicago Vice Commission) as his special "whipping boy." He first addressed himself to the idea that law, to be law, must adhere to *moral principles*. To confine legal action in this way, Lippmann argued, is absurd. Rejecting offhand any contention that valid laws must reflect an objective or transcendent pattern of justice or virtue, he declared: "The object of democracy is not to imitate the rhythm of the stars but to harness political power to the nation's needs." Besides, a moral content for law is meaningless, since "there is nothing so bad but that it can masquerade as moral." Words like liberty, equality, and fraternity—the abstractions of morality—are empty verbiage, serving only as docile horses to be harnessed to any available wagon. Summoning Freudian psychology as his witness, Lippmann argued that the moral shaping of laws is a mere rationalization. What actually happens is the reverse; men consciously or unconsciously shape moral principles to fit what they desire to do. "Words, theories, symbols, slogans, abstractions of all kinds are nothing but the porous vessels into which life flows, is contained for a time, and then passes through. But our reverence clings to the vessels." [8]

The vice commission had also suggested that all laws must be *constitutional*. Again Lippmann was critical. To accept this understanding of law would be, he argued, to make men exist for the sake of the Constitution. By so doing, the Constitution is elevated to the status of an idol and placed alongside "Sanctity of Private Property, Vested Rights, Competition the Life of Trade, Property (at any cost)" as a transient instrument of life which

[7] A *Preface to Politics*, 18.
[8] *Ibid.*, 21, 163, 169.

has been converted into an immutable law of existence. For Lippmann, such an attitude represented a return to classicalism in the
worst sense, with its unwarranted reverence for tradition and its
hostility to change. "Classicalism and invention are irreconcilable
enemies," he proclaimed.[9] If America wished to recapture the
pioneer spirit evidenced in her frontier days, she must free herself
politically from any slavery to historic forms as the standards of
law.

Interestingly enough, in view of Lippmann's pragmatic bias
and his later development, he did not hesitate to quarrel with the
vice commission's additional recommendation that laws should be
reasonable and practical. His objection, as might be suspected, was
to the content of these terms. He wrote, " 'Reasonable' in America
certainly never even pretended to mean in accordance with a rational ideal, and 'practical'—well, one thinks of 'practical politics,'
'practical business men,' and 'practical reformers.' Boiled down,
these words amount to something like this: the proposals must not
be new or startling; must not involve any radical disturbance of any
respectable person's selfishness; must not call forth any great opposition; must look definite and immediate . . ." [10] Such fixation
upon immediate, obvious results did not fit Lippmann's conception
of pragmatic legislation shaped by the long-term needs of human
nature.

What was Lippmann's own standard of legal validity? While he
labored at length to explain it, his ideas still failed to shed their fuz-
ziness. The goal of political action, he maintained, is aesthetic,
not moral—"a quality of feeling instead of conformity to rule."
All laws are but instruments and must be judged in terms of how
effectively they minister "to those concrete experiences which are
as obvious and as undefinable as color or sound." [11] The difficulty
of translating this kind of legal standard into concrete legislation
did not seem to discourage him.

Lippmann's early position reduced itself to this: to be practical

[9] *Ibid.*, 184, 187.
[10] *Ibid.*, 175.
[11] *Ibid.*, 200.

and enforceable, all laws must conform to the unalterable factors of basic human nature. Important as are both power and punishment, they cannot be the real clues to a law's essence; if any law is seriously contrary to the instinctive impulses of the human personality, it will not be long obeyed, regardless of the force marshalled behind it. Nor can laws be fenced in by morality, which is slippery and subjective. As with political institutions, so legal creeds must be fitted "to the wants of men, to satisfy their impulses as fully and beneficially as possible." [12]

It can be objected that, in this kind of discussion, Lippmann was not actually talking about the problem of law *qua* law but, rather, was criticizing the value of particular laws. True, his theory found its starting point in the specific recommendation of one public agency in regard to one set of circumstances. It is also obvious that much of his irritation with the legal process stemmed from the fact that, in the first two decades of this century, American courts were still strongly influenced by nineteenth century, laissez faire thinking. As a result, judicial review tore the heart out of much of the advanced social legislation so dear to the political progressives. The courts were, in the words of Dean Roscoe Pound, "doing nothing, and obstructing everything." [13] Lippmann himself recognized that the real problem was not the power of the courts but the way that power was used;[14] nevertheless, his resentment led him into a wider, though neither profound nor intensive, critique of the whole nature of law.

Lippmann's early legal concepts having been set out in this detail, it is possible to view his development across the next decade or so as a gradual but steady retreat from his initial position. Following World War I Lippmann, as we have seen, made extensive studies of public opinion. As these researches afforded him new perspectives on the practical workings of the democratic process,

[12] *Ibid.*, 84.

[13] Cited in *Drift and Mastery*, 157.

[14] "If the courts made law that dealt with modern necessities, the people would, I believe, never question their power. It is the bad sociology of judges and their class prejudices that are destroying the prestige of the bench." See *Drift and Mastery*, 158.

they also significantly modified his legal understanding. His definition of majority rule as a simple function of power, for instance,
could not help but have implications for any analysis of the enactments of a government operated by majority rule. The first important change in Lippmann's legal philosophy resulted, therefore, when he came to see law not as a reflection of the needs and
drives of instinctive human nature but as the product of a power
conflict. This meant that the essence of law could be found in
the element of coercion. "The prevailing system of rights and duties
at any time is at bottom a slightly antiquated formulation of the
balance of power among the active interests in the community,"
he wrote in 1925. In its naked reality a legal right is a claim someone is able to make successfully; a duty is an obligation someone is
able to impose. As a result, the prevailing laws represent a sort of
modus vivendi for the conflicting interests of society. No genuine
or complete harmony of these interests is attainable (this represented a major retreat from Lippmann's more complacent earlier
views); what is possible is a partial adjustment, so that "the conflicting interests merely find a way of giving a little, and taking a
little, and of existing together without too much bad blood." [15]
Such adjustments are necessary because men must live together
and are, to some degree, dependent upon each other.

Discernible in this type of social theory is the mixed influence
of ideas similar both to those of Thomas Hobbes and those of
John Locke. Like the author of *The Leviathan*, the Lippmann of
the middle 1920's tended to view men finally as isolated individuals, and there was little hint in his thought that human nature
is inherently social or that man is incomplete outside of human
community. Instead, man was pictured as forced into society by
physical circumstances, submitting himself to a rule of law largely
by virtue of the necessity to survive. Still, Lippmann's individualism was never totally Hobbesian, and his understanding of law
included elements of Locke's concept of a community based on
laws as a matter of mutual convenience. Individual men, in real-

[15] *The Phantom Public*, 89–100.

ity, do live in society, and laws are therefore both necessary for survival and convenient for existence.

Despite his refusal to explain the nature of law in Hobbes's simplified terms, Lippmann did assign to working law the primary aspect of coercion. Thus, he wrote, "An established [legal] right is a promise that a certain kind of behavior will be backed by the organized force of the state or at least by the sentiments of the community; a duty is a promise that failure to respect the rights of others in a certain way will be punished." [16] The coercion which gives law its validity may arise from the government, from ecclesiastical codes, from custom, or from habit. The important thing is that a violation is always followed by a penalty of some kind. Viewed in this way, a legal system is the reflection of the relative amount of power each constituent individual or group interest is able to assert.

Though this analysis introduced into Lippmann's thinking the idea of force as the essence of law, it also opened the door to another element—formal validity—which became increasingly important. In a society without law the conflict of interests resolves itself by the use of raw force and often culminates in physical violence or armed warfare. In a civilized society, on the other hand, where ballots are substituted for bullets, power struggles are carried out under accepted rules of procedure, designed to prevent the disasters attendant on violence. Lippmann gradually became convinced of the absolute essentiality of certain democratic procedural rules—such as separation of powers, judicial review, and the presidential veto. His consideration of these matters, however, raised the question of a source for such rules. Lippmann was still far from ready to accept any external standards of moral judgment as a legitimate source, even for procedures. To make them dependent on morality would merely introduce new points of friction: "There are too many moral codes. . . . a political theorist who asks that a local standard be universally applied is merely begging one of the questions he ought to be trying to solve. . . .

[16] *Ibid.*, 100–101.

[namely] the conflict of standards." [17] The only test of rules which Lippmann would accept was a pragmatic one. Rules are judged by their effectiveness in resolving conflicts of interests. If they work, in the sense that they preserve order while securing compliance and facilitating decision, such procedures will normally be acceptable to society. If a rule is evaded or disobeyed by any considerable group of citizens, it is a symptom of the rule's instability and ineffectiveness.

The preeminence of formal rules as summarizing the essence of law was enhanced by the strong note of individualism dominating *A Preface to Morals*. Deeply concerned to protect an area of privacy and freedom for each man, Lippmann asserted that the real law "is neither the accumulated precedents of tradition or a set of commands originating on high which are imposed like orders in an army upon the rank and file below." The importance of this statement is its demonstration that Lippmann had virtually abandoned his earlier contention that law rested ultimately on formal enforcement power. In place of this, he now declared: "The real law in a modern state is the multitudes of little decisions made daily by millions of men." [18]

Once law had been explained in this fashion, it followed that the role of government is not actually to rule men but to aid men in ruling their own affairs. Law is not the order of a traditional sovereign backed by power; it is the complex network of relationships among autonomous individuals, each supreme within his own personal sphere. These relationships can be expressed only in a pattern of procedures—rules which regulate the various relations.

Playing a vital part in the development of this view of law was a special conception of the meaning of sovereignty. The traditional understanding of sovereignty is tenable, Lippmann thought, only in terms of the medieval idea that a sovereign is one who—to use Jean Bodin's definition—"after God, acknowledges no one greater than himself." [19] So long as a ruler's claim to this type of power

[17] *Ibid.*, 30–31.
[18] *A Preface to Morals*, 275.
[19] *Ibid.*, 262.

is effectively undisputed, the description of law as a sovereign's command to his subjects makes sense. Today, however, no such authority actually exists. In a pluralistic, democratic state no unqualified allegiance is given to any governing body or to any individual.

To deal with the revolutionary changes which produced the modern political world, earlier thinkers sought to appropriate the sovereignty principle in a limited government by postulating the idea that the state originated in a social compact between ruler and people; thus, the people were thought of as having delegated their sovereignty, with reservations, to the ruler. From this perspective, law as coercive command could still be made somewhat plausible. In the eighteenth and early nineteenth centuries, as various groups pressed for restrictions on governmental powers in Europe's developing national states, the social contract argument was both popular and useful. Thinkers like Hooker, Milton, Spinoza, Hobbes, Locke, and Rousseau—each in his own way—expounded it. Lippmann observed that "as an historical theory to explain the origin of human society," the whole idea is demonstrably false; yet, "as a weapon for breaking up the concentration of sovereign power and distributing it, the idea has played a mighty role in history." [20]

In the twentieth century, however, the myth of the social contract has largely lost its relevance. "The sovereign, whom it was once desirable to put under contract, has become so anonymous and diffuse that his very existence today is a legal fiction rather than a political fact." [21] In a modern, liberal state, sovereignty resides irretrievably *in* the people and actually cannot be transferred to any legal or political institution, even one created by the people themselves. The phenomenon of "multitudinous mass leadership" has appeared.[22] In such circumstances each man, as his own sovereign, is expected to acquire "the habit of making

[20] *Ibid.*, 266.
[21] *Ibid.*, 267.
[22] Lippmann's understanding in this regard was similar to that advanced by José Ortega y Gasset in *The Revolt of the Masses* (New York, 1932).

judgments instead of looking for orders, of adjusting his will to the wills of others instead of trusting to custom and organic loyalties." [23] In 1929 Lippmann was not frightened by this revolutionary occurrence. He saw it only as a part of an educative process, propelling man toward true maturity. For one thing, loyalty formerly directed to a ruler or to a corporate governing personality would now be forced to turn inward upon the autonomous individual; no external person or structure could claim it. Such internal loyalty could express itself externally only in commitment to a pattern of social conduct or a set of attitudes in politics which corresponded to one's personal attitudes. In practical political terms, this means that a nation of sovereign individuals can give ultimate political loyalty only to a *mode of governing,* expressing itself in normative legal procedures.

How neatly this delineation of sovereignty fitted into the individualistic emphasis of *A Preface to Morals!* The disinterested man, whose guiding maxims for personal conduct are moderation, toleration, and understanding, translates these virtues, politically, into an abiding respect for established law (or procedural norms), for the nonarbitrary character of the democratic process, and for free discussion and rational persuasion in decision-making. The politics of disinterest was thus based not only, as we have previously seen, on a special conception of human nature but also on a complementary understanding of the essence of law.

This type of legal approach, based on form rather than content, was relied on heavily by Lippmann during the thirties. But now and then some signs of doubt emerged. For instance, in the early years of the decade, while arguing for the repeal of the Eighteenth Amendment, he fell back on a line of reasoning remarkably reminiscent of the Lippmann of pre-World War I. Picturing prohibition legislation as "the attempt to impose upon a whole people an absolute rule of personal conduct," he contended that a law which violated the natural appetites of great masses of people could not be enforced. Whether he realized it or not, Lippmann was once again injecting into the meaning of law more than mat-

[23] *A Preface to Morals,* 275.

ters of form. Law, he said, should conform to the will of the people—"the abiding will, not the momentary opinion or the excited whim which propaganda or demagoguery or a spectacular event may arouse." [24]

In another and more important way Lippmann gradually reintroduced significant content into his formal theory of law. By 1934, searching for additional support for the methods of liberal democracy, he discovered that these procedural norms have meaningful historical roots. They gain weight on the basis that they represent a portion of Western man's accumulated wisdom. Lippmann wrote, "The principles of liberalism are not the invention of sentimental theorists. They are the crystallization of years of experience in the government of men. These principles are older than all existing constitutions and are more deeply rooted than any formulation of them that can be put into words." [25]

Though his concern was still for the formal methods of democracy and his appeal to tradition shallow, Lippmann had allowed a larger meaning to find its way into his legal thinking. Historically, democratic roots reach back into a rich resource of philosophical and theological thought about man and his world, and Lippmann was to find that he could not enlist history in defense of democratic procedures without listening to the full testimony of that tradition.

As the thunder of European events warned of impending storms over the United States, the democratic heritage became more and more a matter of concern. Lippmann was forced to realize that his cherished methods of nonarbitrary government were not safely protected from dissolution simply on pragmatic grounds or even by the recognition of their long and honorable tradition. The day after Christmas, 1935, in a solemn newspaper article, he wrote,

[24] "Today and Tomorrow," December 5, 1933.
[25] Lippmann, "In Defense of Liberalism," *Vanity Fair*, XLIII (November, 1934), 24. This sort of statement was in striking contrast to earlier ones by Lippmann. For instance, in 1912 he had written: "You cannot stand pat upon the past. The institutions of the past are like the fresh eggs of the past—good while they were fresh. Society, like each person in it, is a growing, living thing." See "The Most Dangerous Man in the World," 101.

"What is startling in the world today is not that there is so much disorder and unrestrained willfulness, but that large groups of civilized men in almost all countries have come to believe that arbitrariness, rather than law, is right, is noble, is the means by which they must achieve their destiny." [26]

The situation to which Lippmann referred appeared to many to constitute a distinctive phenomenon of the twentieth century— the complete inversion of value standards. The breaking of laws was commonplace, but it was difficult to comprehend how educated, scientifically trained men could acquiesce in an assault on the basic structure of law itself. In Germany, Italy, Russia, and a host of smaller countries this was precisely what was happening. Civilized men were behaving like barbarians. These hard facts compelled Lippmann, along with others of like mind, seriously to rethink their positions concerning the nature of the democratic processes. Was an emphasis on meticulous legal form sufficient?

In that same 1935 newspaper column Lippmann put his stamp of approval on an influential statement written by Professor C. H. McIlwain.[27] McIlwain, an eminent political theorist, saw the great political issue of the time as that between arbitrary government and the special brand of democracy known as constitutionalism. Pure democracy—the unbridled rule of the majority—can produce nothing but eventual disorder, and disorder leads inevitably to tyranny. "In times of disorder," asserted McIlwain, "men care more for order than for liberty." They will, therefore, be tempted to trade their freedom for arbitrary security. To insure the continuance of liberty, a democratic people must put their trust in freedom under law, which means constitutional government. "The powers of our governors should be great, yet must be limited. If so, *Quis custodiet ipsos custodes?* Who is to have an eye on

[26] "Today and Tomorrow," December 26, 1935.

[27] C. H. McIlwain, "Government by Law," *Foreign Affairs*, XIV (1936), 185–98. All quotations in this paragraph are taken from this article. Of it, Lippmann wrote: "If there is such a thing as a list of publications that no one should miss, this article belongs on that list." See "Today and Tomorrow," December 26, 1935.

these governors themselves?" McIlwain's solution was also Lippmann's: there must be "a fearless and impartial interpretation of
law by a free and independent judiciary." McIlwain's article, however, did not go on to face the obvious extensions of the original
question: where does the constitution limiting the ruler derive
its ultimate authority? And what is the people's recourse if the
judiciary ceases to be free, impartial, and independent?

Actually, constitutional theorists were already faced with a concrete situation in which the judiciary had abdicated its function as
a limiting power. The liberal approach to government had been
put to the test in Germany, and neither pragmatic experience nor
tradition had been able to save it. Alarmed, Lippmann thought he
saw in the 1936 proposal by President Franklin Roosevelt to
"pack" the United States Supreme Court the beginnings of the
same type of development. It was against the background of a
world where collectivism had suddenly become a successful rival of
democracy, where individual rights were being swallowed up by
the claims of race and nation, and where democratic processes had
themselves been employed as instruments to abolish personal liberty that Lippmann wrote *The Good Society*.

As Lippmann conceived it in 1937, the problem was specific and
crucial. What had gone wrong with liberalism? What were its fatal
errors? In his grapple with these questions, two major answers
emerged, both of them involving a considerable indictment of
phases of his own past thought. First, he decided, liberalism had
erred when it posited a realm of autonomous individual freedom
requiring no law. Operating from this presumption, nineteenth
century liberals had conceived that the political problem was to
rope off ever-wider areas in which individuals could function
without legal interference—areas in which, essentially, each man
could be a law unto himself. The result was not social harmony
but the static injustices of laissez faire capitalism. Actually, Lippmann charged, no area of life can be free from law, especially in
the highly organized and overlapping patterns of modern civilization. "So the question can never arise whether there should be law

here or no law there, but only what law shall prevail everywhere." [28] In a modern state all rights are sustained by some kind
of law; there is no such thing as a legal vacuum. The individual is
not, cannot be, and refuses to be absolutely autonomous anywhere.

The exposure of this first fallacy of historic liberalism accentu-
ated the second. If there is law everywhere, it must stem from authentic authority. But the liberal democrat attempts to preserve
individual autonomy exactly because he is convinced that nobody
—no king, no aristocracy, no specially trained governing class, no
parliament or congress—is good enough or wise enough to be
trusted with unlimited authority. In a world, all of which is un-
avoidably under authority of one kind or another, how can the
ruling forces be limited? Traditional liberalism, thought Lippmann,
had mistakenly trusted the power of formal legal procedures, separated from the presuppositions which had originally given them
meaning and justification. The lesson of the German experience
was that tyranny and despotism can be installed by strictly legal
methods.

When Lippmann wrote *The Good Society*, a satisfactory answer
to this dilemma of liberalism was still not clear to him. He was
convinced, however, that the liberal democrats had discarded the
most important elements in their own tradition—elements essential to the continuation of freedom within order. They had held to
the forms of liberty, but they had thrown away the content. As one
historical key to the recovery of these essentials, he pointed back
to the moment when the English Chief Justice, Sir Edward Coke,
told King James I that the king was "under God and the law." In
this concept, as it germinated, lay the ideas of constitutionalism in
general and, specifically, of the American Constitution. The
Founding Fathers recognized the unalterable fact that the people
have both the right and the power to rule, but they also knew that
the people require a fundamental law setting out *how* they are to
rule. In a constitutional democracy the *how* of ruling includes
much more than the prescription of procedures; it calls for government operating in the light of basic convictions about the nature

[28] *The Good Society*, 186.

of man. For Lippmann, in 1937, the legal stipulation of the Constitution amounted to the fact that men were required to rule and be ruled according to the cumulative, time-tested traditions of the *common law*.[29]

Since the common law concept was central in Lippmann's thought at this time, it is important not to narrow its meaning more than he intended. He did not point simply to the English law; on the other hand, he was not referring to any special body of ethical rules worked out by philosophers. His conception included the whole body of traditional Western law as it defines individual and social relationships and opens the courts to anyone whose interests have been infringed. This body of law has grown up in the midst of the experience of freedom. Its specific applications can be amended without end, but its core principles cannot be dispensed with. They reflect, even though imperfectly, something universal and absolute.

The principal virtue of this law, as Lippmann saw it, is its insistence on the legal equality of all men: "The lost wisdom of our forefathers was in their discovery . . . that the way to make men free is to replace the decrees and commands of a ruling class by a system of equal laws. . . . They understood that the individual is free in so far as his life is regulated not by the arbitrary commands of other men but by general rules which bind all men alike." [30]

It is necessary to see how this notion differed from what had preceded it in Lippmann's thinking. He spoke now of a law which was general and unchangeable in its validity, applying equally to all men. Such a law did not originate in the arbitrary fiat of any ruler, nor did it mysteriously arise out of the irrational instincts of human beings. The common law "was to be regarded not as the product of any lawgiver, but as the deposit of progressive discovery

[29] Lippmann defined democracy as "the government of the people by a common law which defines the reciprocal rights and duties of persons. The common law is defined, applied, and amended by the representatives of the people." See *The Good Society*, 266.
[30] "Today and Tomorrow," November 25, 1939.

of law *in the very nature of things.*" [31] Law thus finds its essence in its reflection of the nature of reality. This does not mean that the positive law at any given moment is perfect. It cannot therefore be construed as a blind defense of the status quo. Common law in its application to specific situations must be constantly changed and refined. But, at its center, there is a core of abiding truth, and its amendments must operate within the limits set by the nature of reality. The essential content of common law declares the necessity of legal equality and nonarbitrary governing action, principles which involve an understanding of every human being as an "inviolate person."

In a sense, Lippmann's thought from 1913 to 1937 took a circular path; yet, it would be a major mistake to confuse or identify his starting and finishing points. In his early years he argued for a law judged on the basis of content, not form, but this content was conceived in terms of its constructive expression of the irrational, materialistic thrusts of human nature. Deserting this perspective, Lippmann, for a considerable length of time, theorized that law was strictly formal in essence. But, finding the formal dimensions of law inadequate as bastions of an ordered freedom, he eventually returned to an emphasis on content. His idea of content was, however, totally different from that of 1913. In 1937 he argued for a legal content based on a rational understanding of the ideal nature of man, an understanding which had gradually been uncovered during the long pilgrimage of Western culture.

As Lippmann sought to establish the validity of the common law heritage as a supreme legal value, he necessarily found himself involved in a discussion of the relevance of a "higher law." What is the higher law? What is the significance of identifying the essence of law with the nature of reality? Why is man's person inviolable?

The Higher Law

In striking contrast to his later writings, Lippmann, prior to 1929, had little to say about a higher law concept. It was clear, however,

[31] *The Good Society,* 340.

that he put no confidence in human ability to discern any transcendent standard. In 1913, for instance, he declared: "Though a personal vision may at times assume an eloquent and universal language, it is well never to forget that all philosophies are the language of particular men." Human beings, he was convinced, are not equipped to govern in the name of abstract principles— thought to describe eternal, unchanging values—for, in actuality, truth is "a thousand truths which grow and change." [32]

Lippmann's second major book, *Drift and Mastery*, elaborated this theme. Far from espousing any higher law, he diagnosed man's major malady as his failure to adjust to the inexorable disclosure that there is no valid authority outside man himself. In ultimate matters man is autonomous, whether he desires to be or not. So long as he does not realize and accept this, his situation is like that of which Matthew Arnold wrote:

> Nor certitude, nor peace, nor help for pain;
> And we are here as on a darkling plain
> Swept with confused alarms of struggle and flight,
> Where ignorant armies clash by night.[33]

Emancipated from a hierarchically ordered world, modern man drifts until he turns within himself, masters his internal disorder, and then marshals his resources to master the world about him. To seek for any eternal principles, self-evident truths, or higher law is not only cowardice, it is delusion. "The world is not helped much by being told every morning that two and two are four. It is not helped by being told to love men as brothers. Men have been told that for ages." [34]

As Lippmann theorized that all absolutes constitute no more than weapons in man's battle for his own interests, he came close to agreement with the Marxist definition of ideology. What men want, "they come to call God's will, or their nation's purpose." The attempt, therefore, to arrive at universals as working principles of political order is useless, since men's interests vary so enor-

[32] *A Preface to Politics*, "Introduction," unnumbered page six, 121.
[33] Cited in *Drift and Mastery*, 195.
[34] *The Stakes of Diplomacy*, 207.

mously, conflicting drastically, one with another. Where, then, is there any cohesive bond for a political system? Lippmann thought he had discovered such a bond in adherence to a common intellectual method and the supreme importance of objective fact. Under such conditions, "differences may become a form of cooperation and cease to be an irreconcilable antagonism." [35]

This dependence on scientific objectivity as an ordering principle, both personally and in society, was evident in Lippmann's 1920 study of news distortion, *Liberty and the News*. In a chapter entitled "Journalism and the Higher Law," he set forth his conviction that the only law to which a newspaper is ultimately responsible is "to tell the truth and shame the devil." When a newsman departs from this standard, conceiving his task to be one with moral implications—"to keep the nation on the straight and narrow," as Lippmann put it—he is confusing his task with that of "preachers, revivalists, prophets, and agitators." [36] To subordinate truth to edification is to admit that the end justifies the means. While such a doctrine might have been plausible so long as men believed in a benevolent Providence which taught them what end to seek, it is, in this modern world, "blazing arrogance" to elevate moral ends or special purposes to the role of standards.

Behind these confident assertions remained nettling and unsettled questions. In the midst of disclaiming all absolute values as mere human preferences, he had taken his own stand upon at least two values which he presupposed without question to be both absolute and universal: the supremacy of truth and the worth of human personality. Sooner or later, he had to deal with the significance of these propositions. He could argue, as he did in *The Phantom Public*, that "the order which we recognize as good is an order suited to our needs and hopes and habits," [37] thus reducing morality largely to a matter of individual preference. But if every person is actually an end in himself and to himself, and if

[35] "The Basic Problem of Democracy," 627.
[36] *Liberty and the News* (New York, 1920), 13, 7–8.
[37] *The Phantom Public*, 33.

moral values are manifestations of individual or group interests, on what basis could one argue that a person is under obligation to abide by any common standard other than sheer self-centeredness? It is certainly both conceivable and observable that the truth—in terms of raw fact—often conflicts drastically with the interests of particular individuals. What makes truth a higher value than each man's personal desire?

During the period before 1929 Lippmann did not attempt to set out any clear answer to these questions, but it would appear that, in so far as he recognized the problems, his resolution of them moved in two directions. The first involved the highly specu- lative contention that, presumably, all men would desire the ob- jective truth if they could clearly comprehend their own total interests. In addition to positing an ideal and unrealizable condi- tion, this viewpoint also defined truth in the narrow sense of un- adorned fact. The truths with which men deal in actual life are always much more complex. They are facts mingled with and either clarified by or obscured by personal interpretation. In terms of moral action, meaning is far more important than fact. And if meaning, as Lippmann had asserted, is so individual and subjective a matter, then there is no genuine significance in a commitment to truth as an ordering value.

The second direction of Lippmann's thought was vaguely set out, but it is important in terms of what it prefigured. Even this early, there were indications that he saw his own values as obtain- ing force through their reflection of some kind of natural order. That any reference to a fixed natural order from which men could draw moral meaning was contradictory to his whole invective against universals did not seem to bother Lippmann—perhaps be- cause his only specific references to such a possibility were casual and passing. For instance, in a New York *World* editorial, he ar- gued that men ought to visualize themselves as being overwhelmed by the vastness of the solar spaces. In the light of this under- standing, Lippmann asked, of what value is all of man's striving and competition to get ahead in life? "Nothing," he answered his own question, "unless in some measure they have helped to brighten the spirit so that for a brief moment it may reflect *the natural order of the universe.*" [38]

Reference to natural order in this materialistic sense, however, emphasized another difficulty. In a universe the spatial vastness of which makes individual man a puny dot on a minor planet, how can one logically sustain the worth of any one person, or even of the race as a whole? If values are to be drawn solely from what can be discovered in the natural, or material, order of things, man is not seen as the center of value but as peripheral and incidental. Lippmann's escape from this impasse was once more to turn inward, seeking introspectively to derive man's sense of his own value, not from the universe, but from an internal understanding. Men are capable of an ultimate dignity: "they can become aware of themselves, they can make for themselves pictures of their universe, they can find delight and serenity in the thought of them and charity in that for creatures like themselves." [39] Such a description obviously applied to Lippmann's disinterested man, the individual who is, as we have seen, convinced that the world about him is without meaning and who constructed his values through a process of pure introspection. What happens to this man when the force of events around him becomes so strong that it shatters his careful philosophical and psychological defences, Lippmann did not delineate. In 1929 it was no doubt impossible for him to imagine the situations that were to develop, for instance, in the Nazi death camps—situations in which all intellectualized pretences were swept away by the harsh hand of unmitigated evil and totally irrational suffering. Perhaps the snug world of the twenties, still "cushioned and cottoned," did not permit such imagining.

In the face of this trend of thought, one striking article by Lippmann must be mentioned, for it appears to be almost a reverse

[38] Lippmann, "In the Shadow of the Moon," New York *World*, January 24, 1925. Reprinted in Rossiter and Lare (eds.), *The Essential Lippmann*, 127–28. There are no italics in the original.
[39] *Ibid.*

anachronism. A book review of Luigi Sturzo's *Italy and Fascism,* it appeared in *The Commonweal,* a liberal Catholic periodical, in 1927.[40] Sturzo's volume was highly critical of Mussolini's rule, and Lippmann's review was thoroughly sympathetic. He especially agreed with the author's evaluation of the Fascist state: "Fascism, wholly apart from its immediate history in Italy, is the logical and uncompromising development of the autocratic state. . . . There are no rights of man, no rights of the family, no rights of association, lay or spiritual, which are independent of the complete authority of the state."

In opposition to this view Lippmann saw men like Sturzo as representative of a body of doctrine which owed its origin to the teachings of the Catholic Church. Thomas Aquinas laid the foundation for a reverence for natural law, and it is, said Lippmann, to that concept that "all who resist the overweening pretension of the political state have appealed." After pointing out that the supreme philosophical source of Fascist theory was Machiavelli, Lippmann concluded his article with a paragraph that is so out of step with the other expressions of his thought at this stage, and yet so prophetic of his future position, as to warrant quoting in full:

In the modern post-Reformation world, Machiavelli's ideas have won, and in the current political philosophy the state is conceived as "unitary, omnipotent, and irresistible." But there has always been an opposing philosophy in which the state was conceived as one corporation with limited and derived powers, existing among other corporations which were autonomous, and endowed with inalienable rights. If I read history correctly, the world owes this conception to the Catholic thinkers who worked it out in their great conflicts with the kings and nobles. Fundamentally it seems to me the only conception of politics which is consistent with a free and civilized life.

That this endorsement of Roman Catholic thought was somewhat premature became evident in *A Preface to Morals.* In this full exposition of Lippmann's views, no real discussion of natural law

[40] Lippmann, "Autocracy Versus Catholicism," *Commonweal,* V (1927), 527. All quotations in this and the next paragraph are taken from this article.

or inalienable rights appears at all. Aquinas is mentioned only casually, and not always in complimentary fashion.

The idea of disinterestedness was not an original concept with Lippmann.[41] Philosophically, the same basic approach had been developed in varying ways by thinkers like Spinoza, Schopenhauer, and Santayana. As has been noted, it had roots in and resemblances to ancient Stoicism. In one extremely significant way, however, Lippmann's thought strongly departed from classical Stoicism in the direction of Greek Epicureanism. In defining true human maturity, Lippmann declared of man: "But until and unless he feels the vast indifference of the universe to his fate, and has placed himself in the perspective of a cold and illimitable space, he has not looked maturely at the heavens." [42] This picture of the morally neutral universe, indifferent to man's destiny, could not have been accepted by the Stoics. This is an Epicurean concept; that is, it is based on a conviction that the universe operates without discernible purpose and without reference to human wishes or desires. It rejects the Stoic belief in a transcendental goodness to be found in the laws governing reality.[43] It discards any conviction of a destiny which shapes our ends. The Stoic ideas were consciously derived from the major premise: "All is ordered by a superlatively good providence and in playing the parts it assigns us we are doing our utmost to further its design." [44] While Lippmann's

[41] For a discussion of the philosophical background of the concept of disinterestedness, see Annette T. Rubenstein, "Disinterestedness as Ideal and Technique," *Journal of Philosophy*, XXVIII (1931), 461–66.

[42] *A Preface to Morals*, 187.

[43] Cf. these lines from one of the significant documents of Stoic piety, the "Hymn to Zeus" by Cleanthes (b. 330 b.c.). The translation is from F. C. Grant, *Hellenistic Religions: The Age of Syncretism* (New York, 1953), 152f:

> But, Zeus, thou giver of every gift,
> Who dwellest within the dark clouds, wield still
> Thy flashing stroke of lightning, save, we pray,
> Thy children from this boundless misery.
> Scatter, O Father, the darkness from their souls,
> Grant them to find true understanding—
> On which relying thou justly rulest all.

[44] Rubenstein, "Disinterestedness as Ideal and Technique," 463.

description of the mature man's attitude toward pain, suffering, and death might be regarded as Stoic, the motivation of this attitude was plainly Epicurean. The difference lay precisely in a failure to embrace some version of the ancient concept of natural law.

Perhaps it is not amiss to observe, in retrospect, that if (as the 1927 article would indicate) Lippmann was attracted by the intellectual possibilities of Thomistic natural law, and if (as *A Preface to Morals* made clear) he had embraced much of the superstructure of Stoicism while failing to accept its core, it is not surprising that he eventually adopted a natural law position as the basis of his own politics.

From 1930 on, a steadily deepening concern with the relationship between positive law and higher law was characteristic of Lippmann's thought. In late 1931 he declared: "It is the gift of civilized man, the surest mark to distinguish him, that he can at times see through the transient and the complicated to the simple and the certain, that he can live by that vision, and with it master or endure his lot." [45] To fail to discern the permanent behind the passing is to destroy the foundations upon which political structures are erected. Thus, he argued that the development of a constructive political science depends upon the recognition of clear, settled, moral values—values which derive from ancestral tradition, from rational reflection, or from both. "Upon a foundation of merely transient opinions derived from the impression of the moment, undirected by any abiding conception of personal and social values, no influential political science can be constructed, and, it may be, no enduring political state." [46]

As we have seen, the idea that abiding truths might have a philosophical foundation in some concept of natural law had already occurred to Lippmann. During the thirties his conviction that some such understanding of reality must supply men with certainty and assurance grew steadily. He quoted with approval

[45] "Today and Tomorrow," November 12, 1931.
[46] Lippmann, "The Scholar in a Troubled World," *Atlantic Monthly*, CL (August, 1932), 151.

the words of Montesquieu: "I have not drawn my principles from my prejudices but from the nature of things." [47] And he became increasingly certain that the key to a recognition of the true nature of things lay not just in an awareness of contemporary events, but in a study of the whole tradition of man's struggle for self-understanding.

Lippmann's definite avowal of a higher law concept came in *The Good Society*. Because his opinions as to the nature and content of this higher law were still somewhat fluid, his thought remained difficult to pin down. At first, it appeared that what he meant was simply "the spirit of the law," a vague and largely negative idea, born in reaction to the fact that the totalitarians had generally been careful to observe the forms of the law. Toward the close of the book, however, Lippmann positively identified himself with the mainstream of natural law theory. He traced the notion of a higher law back to the Stoics and called it the standard to which all the liberators of mankind had appealed. Discarding completely his earlier disdain for traditional knowledge, he declared that "we are not so full of wisdom, and so comfortably masters of our fate, that we can afford summarily to reject the underlying conception upon which so many sages and saints and heroic leaders have based their hope of a happily ordered existence." [48]

As to the exact content of the higher law, a crucial question remained. Lippmann argued that Blackstone in England and many judges in the United States had made the mistake of identifying higher law with the English common law in its customary application. This enshrined a system of legal particulars without claim to universal relevance. The higher law's genuine substance, maintained Lippmann, is "the denial that men may be arbitrary in human transactions." [49] This is the criterion of all positive law and government. And where is this criterion found? He was now prepared to say that it is progressively discovered by men seeking to achieve a measure of civilization. It is, therefore, a gradual sort of

[47] *The Method of Freedom*, xii.
[48] *The Good Society*, 337.
[49] *Ibid.*, 346.

revelation which can only be appropriated by moving into the stream of the historic Western tradition of law and order.

Even supposing the unlikely possibility that an earlier Lippmann might somehow have found his way to this same set of conclusions, he certainly would have let his case rest at this point. Human beings are persons and must not be treated arbitrarily as things —this he had always believed. That he now labeled this conviction as a higher law, drawn from the nature of things, was not a shocking development. But the Lippmann of 1937 was not content to stop there. *Why* are men persons? *Why* must they be regarded in the light of a nonarbitrary law? Is there, after all, an even higher law than this? Lippmann was obviously still groping for solid ground in his approach to these questions, but he made a brief stab at answering them. Common law, nonarbitrary procedures, traditional equality before the law—these are, after all, only legal mechanisms. They constitute a precarious foundation upon which to build an enduring good society. "It would be mere self-deception to tell ourselves that the disorders into which we have fallen can be overcome by an ingenious programme of laws, policies, measures, and political combinations." [50]

All his life Lippmann had rejected any concept of self-evident truths, holding that modern men must base their political structures on altogether different premises from those held by men in the past. Now he was forced, as he confessed, to ask himself "whether perhaps in reasoning about the problems of our time we had lost vital contact with self-evident truths which have the capacity to infuse the longing to be civilized with universal and inexhaustible energy." The world of free men is in trouble; merely to analyze the sickness and predict the consequences is not enough. Civilization requires direction. If human beings are to preserve their dignity and integrity, they must rediscover some strong philosophical foundations upon which to rest their values. Men must become aware that, inalienably, each person and all persons are inviolate. How can they know this?

[50] *Ibid.*, 371.

The Stoics spoke quietly and in terms intelligible only to an elite. To the masses of the western world the news that all men are more than things was proclaimed by the Christian gospel and was celebrated in its central mysteries. It proclaimed the news to all men that they were not brute things, . . . For in the recognition that there is in each man a final essence—that is to say, an immortal soul—which only God can judge, a limit was set upon the dominion of man over men. . . . The inviolability of the human person was declared.[51]

Walter Lippmann had arrived at a legal understanding which was to remain central in his political theory, providing a necessary basis for his construction of the concept of the public philosophy. He had concluded that the essence of law was not to be discovered in the elements of coercion and punishment, formalism, or the dynamics of human irrationality. Positive law must be viewed in the light of a higher law, a pattern derived both from the true nature of man and his world and from the nature of that moral realm which lies beyond existential man. No definition of law lacking moral and spiritual insight is acceptable. The legal enactments of men and nations are inextricably linked with the "laws of nature and of nature's God." Law must respect the worth of the person, a value ultimately arising out of the status of man as unique in all creation.

[51] *Ibid.*, 372, 378.

The principles of our order are the new principles
which first appeared in the conscience of mankind
a mere two thousand years ago, and this revelation of
man's dignity and of the reign of a higher law and
of the uses of charity is the news, the greatest news,
and perennially the newest news that has ever come
to mankind.

WALTER LIPPMANN

Chapter V

The Relevance of Religion

Perhaps the most striking change of mind revealed by a survey of Lippmann's long intellectual career lies in the area of religion's relevance to politics. In this regard it is possible, if one is only slightly arbitrary, to chop his life and thought into vividly contrasting segments, with the dividing line coming shortly after the publication of *A Preface to Morals* in 1929. During the first of these two periods Lippmann's writings revealed hostility, disdain, almost contempt toward virtually all forms of religious commitment and especially toward organized religion, while the latter period evidenced a steadily growing appreciation, both for the churches and for the broad structure of Christian belief.

Whether Lippmann's mature political philosophy can legitimately be classed as Christian in terms of presuppositions and orientation is an important question. The judgment must be made against the background of the changing patterns of his long-term religious outlook.

Lippmann's Religious Development

While it is difficult to piece together any detailed account of Lippmann's personal religious pilgrimage without indulging in unwar-

121

ranted speculation, certain important events and shifts of attitude can be singled out. That he grew up in a liberal Jewish home with what appears to have been a minimal religious connection has already been set out. His reaction against Judaism, perhaps inspired more by social and cultural considerations than by doctrinal ones, seems to have come at a fairly early age. After he entered Harvard, there is no further evidence of any formal identification with a synagogue. In his writings Judaism is largely ignored, with the exception of one important article which appeared in *The American Hebrew* in 1922.[1] In this article at least one clear clue to Lippmann's personal religious stance can be discovered. Addressing himself to the problems created by Jewish stereotypes, he offered this advice: "Because the Jew is conspicuous, he is under all the greater obligation not to practice the vices of our civilization. He needs more than anyone else to learn the classic Greek virtue of moderation; for he cannot, even if he wishes, get away unscathed with what less distinguishable men can." [2] This statement underscored Lippmann's own commitment by pointing his fellow Jews not to the piety of the Old Testament but to the "classic Greek virtue of moderation." Whatever else the article might have revealed about his psychological reactions to his Jewish heritage, it clearly demonstrated that he had broken his intellectual ties with Judaism, being oriented instead toward the humanistic outlook associated with Greek thought.

If Lippmann's early attitude toward his own religious background was one of rejection, his opinion of Christian churches and beliefs was no more favorable. Early in life he appears to have acquired a distaste for Christianity in its popular form. In an interesting passage in *Drift and Mastery*, he recounted a childhood incident which evidently left a deep impression. Having misbehaved at a birthday party, he was lectured by a maid "in a solemn voice," while "the flickering shadows on the cake-strewn carpet were un-

---

[1] For a summary and evaluation of this article see Heinz Eulau, "From Public Opinion to Public Philosophy," *American Journal of Economics and Sociology*, XV (1956), 439–51.

[2] Cited in *ibid.*, 444.

bearable and accusing shapes full of foreboding to boys lost in sin." The effect on young Lippmann was traumatic: "I burst into tears at the impending wrath of God. And for years God was the terror of the twilight." [3]

As is so often the case, religion and sex were irrationally inter-twined in Lippmann's adolescent thinking. In *Drift and Mastery* he vigorously condemned parents who made of sex a "bogey" for their children. The young child inquires about his birth. "For an-swer he is given lies and a sense of shame; for ever afterwards he too lies and is ashamed. And so we begin to build up the sense of sin and the furtiveness of sex." [4] Lippmann's prescription of frank sex education as a cure-all for problems of sexual misconduct and guilt was typical of the progressive thought of the times. Clearly, he blamed the churches for much of contemporary society's failure in this area. Religious people were conditioned to think of morality in almost exclusively sexual terms, and, even more perversely, the method of the taboo was their recommended device for controlling evil. "The Puritans," he wrote, "tried to choke the craving for pleasure in early New England. They had no theaters, no dances, no festivals. They burned witches instead." Lippmann's concen-tration on this aspect of religion led him to assert that "the very sex impulse, so largely degraded into vice, is the dynamic force in religious feeling." [5] Throughout *A Preface to Politics* there was the underlying suggestion that, if only the sexual impulses could be cleanly and constructively liberated, both in their physical expres-sions and in their sublimations, the need for religion as such might well disappear.

Lippmann was, of course, a disciple of William James, and he had predictably good words to say about James's influential vol-ume, *The Varieties of Religious Experience*. Obviously, however, the disciple was neither as tolerant nor as open-minded as the teacher. The objective investigations demanded by James auto-matically destroyed, thought Lippmann, any special religious pre-

[3] *Drift and Mastery,* 241–42.
[4] *Ibid.,* 245.
[5] *A Preface to Politics,* 43, 149.

tensions. With approval he quoted Santayana: "The gods are demonstrable only as hypotheses but as hypotheses they are not gods." [6] Pragmatically, Lippmann could see that traditional faith had served certain purposes in the past, but as an intelligent modern man, unable to take the ultimate claims of religious faith seriously, he himself rejected completely all supernatural doctrine. He was, indeed, angry because he felt that Christianity and, especially, the Roman Catholic Church had, historically, blocked man's progress toward maturity in order to maintain its power: ". . . the Church was not content to meet needs and compensate weakness. It tried to make weakness permanent. In other words, the Church used all its tremendous power over men to keep them wanting that which the Church could give." [7]

This type of criticism was typical of Lippmann's early sociological indictment of the churches. He saw them as defenders of the status quo, cradles of conservatism and reaction. Assaying the historical role of religious organizations, he commented somewhat sarcastically: "Of course, the Church was no aid to the inventor or to anyone who was really extending the bounds of human power. Of course, it was hostile to democracy and to every force that tended to make people self-sufficient." As an institution shackled by tradition and self-interest, the modern church is singularly inadequate to give moral guidance. He wrote, "No wonder the churches are empty. . . . Ministers are as bewildered as the rest of us, perhaps a little more so. For they are expected to stand up every week and interpret human life in a way that will vitalize feeling and conduct. And for this work of interpretation they have the simple rules of a pastoral people. . . . If the churches really could interpret life they would be unable to make room for the congregations . . . ." [8]

There are no signs that Lippmann's general attitude toward religion and the churches changed in any material way until after the publication of A Preface to Morals. In the little he wrote in this

[6] Drift and Mastery, 299.
[7] Ibid., 204.
[8] Ibid., 204, 155–56.

area during the twenties he continued to maintain an iconoclastic stance toward traditional faith, occasionally berating the churches for their failures in moral training,[9] and strongly advocating the thesis that orthodox religious systems and democratic self-government are basically incompatible in the modern world. His arguments led him to the conclusion that religiously disposed societies are most susceptible to authoritarian government, while the industrialized, less religious nations of the world are the favorable areas for political freedom. What is true of nations is also true of individuals. Those persons who have attained a high measure of maturity no longer require the props of religious faith; they are able to accept reality's variety and tentativeness. "The only people who can stomach a pluralistic philosophy are those who in some way or another have grown strong enough to do without an absolute faith." [10]

One striking new factor underlay the entire structure of A Preface to Morals, however, and it signaled a turning point in Lippmann's moral and religious philosophy. Stressing in his earlier writings the progressive destruction of vital religious faith by science and technology, he had always viewed this phenomenon as a thoroughly healthy development. In Drift and Mastery he had written: "Life has overflowed the little systems of eternity. Thought has become humbler because its task is greater. We can invoke no monumental creeds, because facts smile ironically upon them. And so in a changing world, men have cast aside the old thickset forms of their thinking for suppler experimental ones. They think oftener. They think more lavishly, and they don't hang their hope of immortality on the issue of their thoughts." [11] By the time A Preface to Morals was penned, his optimistic disdain for and even rejoicing over the collapse of religious vitality had been replaced by a deep-felt concern for the destructive consequences of religious indifference. In one sense, his whole book can be viewed

[9] Cf., Lippmann, "Cecilia Cooney," editorial in the New York World, May 8, 1924. Reprinted in Rossiter and Lare (eds.), The Essential Lippmann, 444–45.

[10] Drift and Mastery, 203.

[11] Ibid., 207–208.

as a profound attempt to repair the ravages wreaked in his own soul by the "acids of modernity." The personal dimensions of his philosophy are obvious in the opening sentences: "Among those who no longer believe in the religion of their fathers, some are proudly defiant, and many are indifferent. But there are also a few, perhaps an increasing number, who feel that there is a vacancy in their lives. This inquiry deals with their problem." [12] It is not amiss to apply Lippmann's classification to his own career. In the headstrong days at Harvard and immediately afterwards, he had been "proudly defiant" in his rejection of religion. The early years of the twenties seem to have been a time of relative indifference, for he had little to say, one way or another, about religion. But by 1929 he was existentially constrained to deal with a spiritual "vacancy" in his own life.

But if Lippmann had become aware of the essential role of religious faith in personal life, this did not mean that he was prepared to move in the direction of any recognizably Christian position. He was still hostile, for instance, to organized Christianity. As Edmund Wilson observed in his famous review of A Preface to Morals, "What Walter Lippmann is engaged in demonstrating in the first part of this book is that the churches have become impossible." [13] This judgment applied to the churches even in their most liberal or "modernist" manifestations. While Lippmann was highly critical of traditional orthodoxy, he was, interestingly enough, more specific and crushing in his condemnation of modern attempts to adapt Christianity to contemporary thought patterns. His severest criticisms were reserved not for J. Gresham Machen, the fundamentalist, but for Harry Emerson Fosdick and Kirsopp Lake, outstanding liberal leaders.[14]

[12] A Preface to Morals, 3.
[13] Edmund Wilson, "Antidote to Despair," New Republic, LIX (1929), 210.
[14] Cf. A Preface to Morals, 21–36. This same tendency in Lippmann is evident in his Barbour–Page Lectures at the University of Virginia in 1928. In these lectures he attempted to present a Socratic discussion between a religious fundamentalist and a "modernist." In seeking to put in the mouth of each imaginary speaker the most logical and convincing case, he suc-

What distressed Lippmann about the decay of orthodox religion was not the spiritual, other-worldly consequences for men (consequences whose validity he did not accept), but an experimental realization of the necessity for some center of authority around which to organize life. "For the modern man who has ceased to believe, without ceasing to be credulous, hangs, as it were, between heaven and earth, and is at rest nowhere." [15] What Lippmann attempted was to construct for himself and for others of like mind a secular religion. In a sense, he paralleled William James's attempt to find a moral equivalent for war by seeking to derive a moral equivalent for religion. While condemning the artificial faiths of men—such substitutes for orthodoxy as the religions of nature, progress, science, and patriotism—he paradoxically offered in their stead a similar synthetic, a religion based on the Utopian individual who had learned to be his own perfect master, never desiring anything except what he ought to desire. His proposal was an extension of his early demand for a science of human nature. The words of an unfriendly critic are exaggerated, but in them is a modicum of truth: "His solution confused education with obedience training, and became freedom through the servitude of conditioned reflexes." [16]

Lippmann's ersatz religion was a type of humanism offered to those who could not accept the "grandiose fiction" of a supernatural kingdom. "When men can no longer be theists, they must, if they are civilized, become humanists." [17] He saw a humanistic

---

ceeded in outlining a much more cogent argument on the fundamentalist side of the dialogue than on the liberal side. See *American Inquisitors*.

[15] *A Preface to Morals*, 9.

[16] David C. Phillips, "Walter Lippmann and the New Philosophies, 1910–1935." (Honors paper, Williams College, 1958), 62–63.

[17] *A Preface to Morals*, 137. Elsewhere, Lippmann has defined humanism as follows: "There never has been a strict doctrine of humanism. . . . The meaning of humanism has been determined by the usage of six centuries. . . . It is the name of a human attitude which revived in Europe about 1300 and it signifies the intention of men to concern themselves with the discovery of a good life on this planet by the use of human faculties." See Lippmann, "Humanism as Dogma," *Saturday Review of Literature*, VI (1930), 817–19. For critical considerations of Lippmann's humanism,

faith as pragmatic in nature, since it demonstrates itself in human experience. It is rational and relevant, based on the surest available knowledge of the conditions of human happiness.

From the humanism of A Preface to Morals to the declarations of the last pages of The Good Society is a long step. The rapid modification of Lippmann's religious views in the decade following 1929 must be understood in terms of the drastic pressure of world events—plus the probability of an increasing realization of the inadequacy of some, though not all, phases of the philosophy of disinterestedness. The exact extent to which he changed his personal religious views remains problematical, but it is clear that his attitude toward the churches altered drastically. One senses the depth of the shift by reading Lippmann's address to a dinner initiating a 1938 Salvation Army fund drive: "The final faith by which all human philosophies must be tested, the touchstone of all party creeds, all politics of state, all relations among men, the inner nucleus of the universal conscience, is in possession of the Salvation Army." This was the same Lippmann who had written in A Preface to Morals: "This is the first age, I think, in the history of mankind when the circumstances of life have conspired with the intellectual habits of the time to render any fixed and authoritative belief incredible to large masses of men." That it was the same man, and not some totally transformed saint, did become clear as Lippmann went on to explain the "final faith" in terms still strongly flavored with humanism. Yet his eventual summary of the principle gave evidence of the direction in which his thought was moving: "On the banners of this organization are inscribed the declaration on which all human decency depends, the declaration that the soul of man is of infinite worth and so ultimately inviolable." [18]

Not many months before his Salvation Army speech, Lippmann had penned a moving and significant tribute to Amelia Earhart, the American woman flyer who had disappeared in the course of a

see Morrow, "Religion and the Good Life"; and Shailer Matthews, "The Religious Basis of Ethics," Journal of Religion, X (1930), 222–31.

[18] Address to Salvation Army dinner, New York, March 22, 1938, reported in New York Herald-Tribune (March 23, 1938), 21.

trans-Pacific flight. He characterized Miss Earhart as one who had helped make the world a better place in which to live through her daring and courage. In classifying her with "the heroes, the saints and seers, the explorers and the creators" Lippmann concluded: "No preconceived theory fits them. No material purpose actuates them. They do the useless, brave, noble, the divinely foolish and the very wisest things that are done by man. And what they prove to themselves and to others is that man is no mere creature of his habits, no mere automaton in his routine, no mere cog in the collective machine, but that in the dust of which he is made there is also fire, lighted now and then by great winds from the sky." [19] What is the "fire" in man which somehow transcends the dust? And whence came the "great winds from the sky"? Poetically and figuratively, Lippmann was arguing for dimensions of reality and meaning which reach beyond the mundane experiences of men. And more and more clearly he came to sense that it was this same insistence on the importance of a realm of ultimate value which constituted the heart of the message of Western religion.

Lippmann's new appreciation for religion extended beyond the bounds of its historic witness to transcendent reality to the churches in general. In 1936, reviewing the history of democratic success in the United States, he concluded that much of the practical achievement was due to the fact that "there have existed independent institutions and independent men. Foremost . . . has been the judiciary. . . . But the judiciary has not stood alone. . . . There have been others, notably the free churches." [20] And, in 1939, in a revealing newspaper column he wrote words which carry more than a hint of autobiographical significance:

In the popular philosophy which comes down to us from the eighteenth century it was, on the whole, assumed that religion and patriotism were opposed to freedom and democracy . . . ; thus, until very recently, the progressive democrat was almost invariably a pacifist in favor of disarmament, an internationalist who distrusted national pa-

[19] "Today and Tomorrow," July 8, 1937.
[20] Lippmann, "The Deepest Issue of Our Time," *Vital Speeches of the Day*, II (1936), 603.

triotism, and a tolerator of religion who in his heart believed that science would supplant it.

It has been demonstrated first in central Europe and then in the democracies of Western Europe that to dissociate free institutions from religion and patriotism is to render them unworkable and . . . defenseless. It has been shown that the final resistance to tyranny in all the totalitarian regimes has been made by devoutly religious churchmen who alone had a conviction which made them see that resistance to tyranny is obedience to God.[21]

The personal process by which Lippmann moved from the wholesale rejection of the classical religious tradition to an appreciative evaluation of the Greco-Judaeo-Christian heritage has not been distinguished by doctrinal apologetic. His works show few intimations of any serious intellectual struggle to overcome strictly theological difficulties. Why this is true will be explored somewhat in the second portion of this chapter. But, if one pieces together the hints which are given in *The Good Society*, he will see that Lippmann's reasonings moved along a decidedly practical and pragmatic road. The detailed analysis of collectivism and its threat to liberal democracy, which makes up the bulk of the 1937 volume, led him, he wrote, "to the realization that however bitterly they [the collectivists] may fight each other, they are all in rebellion against the moral heritage of Western society, and that upon the foundations of that heritage men must make their stand against another relapse into barbarism." This much he had apprehended even before he began writing his book. In the course of his work on the manuscript, however, he moved beyond this. He considered the historically incontrovertible fact that the founders of free democratic political institutions had drawn both their courage and their inspiration from truths declared to be self-evident. Such an observation constituted a personal stumbling block for Lippmann for, as he confessed, "I had grown up in an age when it was said that there were no self-evident truths." [22]

As he began work on the final, constructive sections of *The Good Society*, Lippmann became concerned with reanalyzing

[21] "Today and Tomorrow," January 7, 1939.
[22] *The Good Society*, 330, 372.

the history of liberal democracy in a new attempt to uncover its essence. Pushing past his own now-recognized "prejudices and un-examined notions," he sought a "final rampart" where men might take their stand for freedom. His reflection led him to the con-clusion that the vital difference between political slavery and free-dom rested in the valuation placed by the state and society on man as a person. In Western culture, as the specific relationships of men in society have been progressively defined by law, a basic truth has emerged: ". . . something is left over—a residual essence in each man which is not at anyone's disposal. That essence becomes au-tonomous. And so out of the slave, who was a living person treated as a thing, there emerges a person who is no longer a thing." [23]

Such a concept is not, uniquely, either a Christian or, in general, a religious idea. It can be and has been held by agnostic human-ists. Consciously or unconsciously, Lippmann himself had op-erated with something closely akin to this view from the begin-ning. Now, however, the concept began to assume new dimensions. In the late thirties Lippmann became deeply impressed by the fact that the collectivists, especially the European totalitarians, were so bitter in their attacks upon religion. There was, he decided, a mean-ing in this circumstance:

Collectivist regimes are always profoundly irreligious. For religious ex-perience entails the recognition of an inviolable essence in men; . . . By the religious experience the humblest communicant is led into the presence of a power so much greater than his master's that the dis-tinctions of this world are of little importance. So it is not accident that the only open challenge to the totalitarian state has come from men of deep religious faith. For in their faith they are vindicated as immortal souls, and from this enhancement of their dignity they find the reason why they must offer a perpetual challenge to the dominion of men over men.[24]

Thus, Lippmann had moved to the point of identifying the high evaluation of man's personhood as an idea with distinctive religious roots which arises from the religious man's conviction that he is a being created by God and endowed with an immortal soul.

[23] *Ibid.*, 373–75.
[24] *Ibid.*, 382.

If such a concept is, as he had come to believe, the core of liberal democracy, there exists an unseverable connection between the religious heritage of the West and its political freedom.

The next decisive step for Lippmann was to associate this truth more definitely with a specific religious tradition. This is not to say that he moved toward a narrow or exclusivist version of Christian doctrine. The ideas of inviolate personhood and an ultimate, unchangeable structure of moral reality are for Lippmann part of "the nature of things"—the way things are. Wherever and however this structure of being is uncovered, it remains truth. Thus, Lippmann did not hesitate to link Mahatma Gandhi with St. Paul as a man "transformed in the renewing of his mind . . . not 'conformed to this world.'" His description of Gandhi was significant, as he classified the Mahatma among the "seers": "The insight of the seers . . . is vertical: They deal, however wide their appeal, with each person potentially, as he might be transformed, renewed, and regenerated. And because they appeal to experience which men have not yet had, with things that are not at hand and are out of their immediate reach, with the invisible and the unattained, they speak and act, as Gandhi did, obscurely, appealing to the imagination by symbolic evocation and subtle example." [25]

Within the traditions of his own culture, however, Lippmann now conceded that these crucial evaluations of the human person and of the structure of reality found their strongest, clearest expression in historic Christianity. When Pope Pius XI died in 1939, Lippmann paid tribute to him as the exponent of an indispensable idea: "This idea is the mold in which Western civilization has been formed. It is that because he [man] is endowed with reason and can, therefore, choose between falsehood and truth, man is an inviolable soul; that because he is an inviolable soul, man must never be treated as if he were a thing; and he can never finally surrender to arbitrary unreason and brute force." This concept is "that faith which, despite all the political and sectarian

[25] "Today and Tomorrow," February 3, 1948.

and dogmatic differences that divide them, is the basic and universal faith of Western men." [26]

Since 1939 Lippmann has continued to operate from this essential stance toward religion, and it is this structure which is evident in *The Public Philosophy*. Some summary observations can be ventured about his religious position at the present time, in so far as he has publicly expressed it.

First, Lippmann's thought is difficult to classify according to any standard theological category. He can be viewed as, in some sense, a theist, since his argument for man's value as a unique created entity presupposes the reality of an ultimate "ground of being," standing in some sense over against man. This judgment seems to be substantiated by a number of statements in *The Public Philosophy*. Here, in 1955, Lippmann identified the rise of the so-called "death of God" philosophical movement as a disturbing development. He used Jean-Paul Sartre, the French existentialist, as an example of modern atheism. Sartre, following Nietzsche, declares that "God is dead." Lippmann observed: "The critical point is not that he refuses to believe in the existence, however attenuated, of an anthropomorphic God. There can be, indeed there is, great faith and deep religion without any concrete image of God." But Sartre's radical unbelief goes much deeper. He has done away "with the recognition that beyond our private world there is a public world to which we belong." He refuses to believe that "behind the metaphors and the sacred images, there is any kind of independent reality that can be known and must be recognized." [27] Lippmann sees the certainty of an objective, abiding essence of reality beyond the reach of man's manipulation—the conviction against which Sartre's attack is launched—as the central core of the Western heritage. To this conviction Lippmann himself subscribes, and it does not disturb him to apply the traditional title, *God*, to this objective structure of truth.

In a loose meaning of the word this stance can be labeled

[26] "Today and Tomorrow," February 11, 1939.
[27] *The Public Philosophy*, 134–35.

"theism." But if one describes "theism" in traditionally orthodox terms, he includes a more complex set of beliefs. Concepts of God as personal, as supernatural, and as known by revelation enter into the picture. There is no evidence that Lippmann has chosen to attach any of these traditional descriptions to the objective reality he designates as "God." His classification as a "theist" is, therefore, hazy. Clearly, Lippmann cannot be dropped into any customary Christian pigeonhole. Because of his espousal of a concept of natural law, some observers have automatically and, perhaps, wishfully assumed that Lippmann has become a Roman Catholic. This is not true.[28] Following the publication of *The Good Society* in 1937, it became customary for many Catholic writers to refer to Lippmann in favorable terms and, in some cases, to read into his publications deeper affinity for Catholicism than was actually present. As Lippmann specifically identified the heart of the Western cultural heritage with an historic stream that included the early Church Fathers and Thomas Aquinas, this tendency became more widespread. L. J. A. Mercier, for example, writing in *Commonweal*, seemed to imply that in some sense Lippmann's entire philosophic position was virtually that of the Catholic Church.[29] Sometime shortly after World War II, Walter Winchell, the columnist, gave credence to a rumor that Lippmann was on the verge of formal entrance into Catholicism—a report which Lippmann categorically denied.

In 1951 a survey by Warren Allen Smith for *The Humanist* magazine included letters to prominent authors inquiring about their attitude toward humanism as a philosophy of life. Lippmann seems not to have answered many of Smith's specific questions, but he did observe that such comments as those of Professor Mercier were based entirely on his published work and "constitute, as I understand it, his interpretation of what I wrote in *The*

[28] In a letter to the author, dated March 31, 1964, Lippmann wrote: "I have not formally identified myself with any church."

[29] See L. J. A. Mercier, "Walter Lippmann's Evolution," *Commonweal*, XXX (1939), 348–50. See also an editorial, "Spiritual Revolution," *Commonweal*, XXIII (1936), 533–34; and L. J. A. Mercier, "Columnists and Professors," *Commonweal* (1940), 296–98.

Good Society." [30] Lippmann denied that there had been any recent radical change in his fundamental religious views. On the basis of this reply Smith classified Lippmann as in sympathy with the position of "Naturalistic Humanism," but his judgment in this regard is open to serious question. What can be said with certainty is that Lippmann has attempted to fit a growing conviction of some type of theistic reality into the essentially humanist structure of his earlier years. In a conversation with David Weingast in 1946, Lippmann indicated that he still holds, in general, to the ethical position developed in *A Preface to Morals*, but that he now recognizes that "right and wrong are not transitory" but are, rather, "inherent in the nature of things." [31] Lippmann's humanistic outlook and scale of values have, in effect, sought to find for themselves some enduring base on which to rest for ultimate justification.

The problem of classifying Lippmann religiously is pointed up by the difficulty of determining what he means when he employs terminology ordinarily associated with theological concepts. His later writing is replete with religious language—words like "repentance," "salvation," "faith," and "revelation." One cannot be certain, however, that when Lippmann employs these terms he means them to be understood in any normative Christian sense. A case in point is his use of the word "revelation." The inviolability of man as a created person is, he often asserts, a revelation which has gradually come to man across the centuries of his struggle for civilization. Does this mean that the objective structure of ultimate reality has, in some way, reached out toward man —as the historic Christian faith asserts—to reveal to him that which he could not have discovered for himself? When questioned, Lippmann's answer is significant, though still not totally clear. He writes, "Although I myself do not think that knowledge of the realm of the spirit can be acquired *only* by revelation, I respect those who feel they have acquired it that way. I believe in man's

[30] Cited in Warren Allen Smith, "Authors and Humanism," *The Humanist*, XI (1941), 199.

[31] Weingast, *Walter Lippmann*, 107.

progressive discovery *by using his own resources.*"[32] What he seems to be saying is that he believes in an objective spiritual reality but that he conceives this reality to be essentially passive, waiting to be uncovered by man's use of his reason and spiritual intuition. This is surely a type of theistic humanism, but one which carries with it discernible undertones of eighteenth century deism. Perhaps it is fair to say that it is not only Lippmann's political philosophy but also his religion which show vital similarities to that of the American Founding Fathers.

The Concept of Myth

Surprisingly, most analyses of Walter Lippmann's political theory have overlooked the continuing importance of his understanding of myth and symbol.[33] Anyone cognizant of the major currents of contemporary theological thought and controversy must, however, be sensitive to any role myth might play in a pattern of philosophical thought.

In recent years the understanding of myth has assumed profound importance in theology. Most modern theologians and historians of religion use the word "myth" as a technical term for that literary form in which other-worldly matters are framed in this-worldly concepts. "Thus, myth expresses truth in a hidden or indirect language, not in an open and direct way."[34] Events of the past can, generally speaking, be religiously significant for the present only as they are lifted out of their specific context of occurrence and translated into symbols of universal situations. To perform this translation is the function of myth. In a lucid presentation it has been pointed out by Ernst Cassirer that myth arises out of an activity of the human mind or psyche distinct from, and

[32] Lippmann to the author, March 31, 1964. The italics are mine.

[33] Only in a paper by an Amherst College student have I found any consideration, for instance, of the influence of Georges Sorel on Lippmann's early thought. See Robert D. Kuklis, "The Democratic Faith of a Young Intellectual" (Typescript in Lippmann Collection, Yale University Library).

[34] E. Dinkler, "Myth," *The Interpreter's Dictionary of the Bible*, K–Q, 487.

independent of, that which produces philosophy or speculative thought. "Myth does not arise solely from intellectual processes; it sprouts forth from deep human emotions." [35] By many thinkers myth is seen as a vehicle for the conveyance of truths that can be adequately expressed in no other way. Existential realities concerning man, his world, and the nature of the spiritual realm well up in myth as in nothing else. Thus, myths become indispensable for the conceptualization of spiritual truth.

There is no evidence that this sophisticated modern understanding was present in Lippmann's early thought. Obviously, however, some general idea of myth had entered his arsenal of political concepts, at least by the time he wrote A Preface to Politics in 1913. As Lippmann sought to deal with the problem of creeds, both moral and political, he argued for the application of a pragmatic test. Creeds are not important on the basis of their accuracy in reflecting objective reality but in proportion to their practical value as incentives to action: "It is more penetrating, in my opinion, to ask of a creed whether it served than whether it was true.' " [36] Creeds are instruments of the will; they can be evaluated only in terms of the purposes they serve. They are adequate instruments in terms of their relevance to the basic thrusts and irrational desires of human personality.

As a typical example of such a creed, or, more accurately, such a "social myth," Lippmann pointed to the idea of the social contract. Rousseau's theory cannot be accurately viewed in a detached, objective manner which passes judgment on its historical truth or falsity. "Jean-Jacques is in fact a supreme case—perhaps even a slight caricature—of the way in which formal creeds bolster up passionate wants." [37] The social contract theory illustrates a basic human category, an idea which, while objectively untrue, is of the highest practical importance.

In 1913 Lippmann felt that the political thinker who most clearly recognized this truth was the French Syndicalist, Georges

[35] Ernst Cassirer, The Myth of the State (New Haven, 1946), 43.
[36] A Preface to Politics, 225.
[37] Ibid., 226.

Sorel. Many contemporary observers had labeled Sorel's idea of the "social myth" as a "silly paradox," but Lippmann was impressed by Sorel's reasoning. The Syndicalists advocated a General Strike—a total stoppage of all labor processes within a nation —as the decisive battle of the class struggle and the core of the Socialist movement. When told by Fabians like Sidney Webb that the General Strike was an immature and naive concept, an idle dream which could never actually take place, Sorel's response was startling. He admitted that the strike could never actually occur; it was simply a "myth." But this fact was essentially irrelevant. He explained, "A knowledge of what . . . myths contain in the way of details which will actually form part of the history of the future is . . . of small importance; they are not astrological almanacs; it is even possible that nothing which they contain will ever come to pass. . . . The myth must be judged as a means of acting on the present; any attempt to discuss how far it can be taken literally as future history is devoid of sense. It is the myth in its entirety which is alone important."

Sorel understood that a myth is to be judged in terms of its adequate expression of the aspirations of men. "By means of [myths] . . . it is possible to understand the activity, the feelings and the ideas of the masses preparing themselves to enter on a decisive struggle; the myths are not descriptions of things, but expressions of a determination to act." [38] As examples of the effectiveness of great myths Sorel cited primitive Christianity, the Reformation, the French Revolution, and the Mazzini campaign in Italy. Lippmann agreed, commenting: "The myth is not one of the outgrown crudities of our pagan ancestors. We, in the midst of our science and our rationalism, are still making myths, and their force is felt in the actual affairs of life." As a contemporary political myth in the making, he pointed to Theodore Roosevelt's grandiloquent announcement in the 1912 presidential campaign, "We stand at Armageddon and we battle for the Lord." [39]

[38] Georges Sorel, *Reflections on Violence*, trans. T. E. Hulme and J. Roth (Glencoe, Ill., 1950), 143–53, 57.
[39] *A Preface to Politics*, 230.

Lippmann saw Sorel's concept of myth as an extension of William James's "will to believe." In the myth, however, the emphasis is not on man's ability to use belief as a guide but on the pragmatic efficiency of a motivating force. Sorel's "social myth" organized and directed man's aspirations toward a definite end. What mattered was that the myth must express men's desires so completely that they would be willing to act decisively. Lippmann was not at all convinced that Sorel's General Strike was the answer for society's problems; instead he had his own "social myth" —the idea that man can prove himself the total master of the material universe, that he is a creator and not a creature, and that society is made for man's uses.

Lippmann's early understanding of myth did not come from Sorel alone. From differing perspectives other twentieth century thinkers had discovered the same truth. A special example was Freud, whose analysis of "the abracadabra of our dreams" contributed much to a realization of the power of fantasy in human motivation.[40] The thinker who had stated this insight most provocatively, however, was Friedrich Nietzsche. In *Beyond Good and Evil* the German philosopher had declared that "the falseness of an opinion is not for us any objection to it." [41] The power of an idea is far more important than the factual truth. What Nietzsche had done, thought Lippmann, was to lay bare the abstract pretensions of all creeds, revealing them as dogmatic instruments of human purpose.

For Lippmann in 1913, Christianity fitted neatly into the classification of myth. He accepted Sorel's description of primitive Christianity as primarily shaped by the myth of an impending Second Coming and the resultant end of the world. Lippmann went on to describe the Christian myth as having demonstrated its failure in modern times, since it no longer adequately incarnated human desire. Many of the liberal churches had actually recognized this fact and had sought to revitalize their ministries in

[40] *Ibid.*, 233. See also Lippmann, "An Epic of Desire," *New Republic*, VII (1916), 21–22.
[41] Cited in *A Preface to Politics*, 234.

terms of human reality. In turning to civic reform or to socialism, as so many had done, however, the churches were abandoning the original myth which had given them birth. "They may continue to practice some of its moral teachings and hold to some of its creed, but the Christian impulse is for them no longer active. A new dream, which they reverently call Christianity, has sprung from their desires." [42]

As we have seen, one aspect of Lippmann's developments across the decade and a half after 1913 was a retreat from his initial conviction of the nature of man as fundamentally irrational. In this process myth lost much of its attraction for him. Rather than as an indirect expression of truth about man's basic self, he saw myth primarily as a propaganda technique to be criticized. As early as *Drift and Mastery* (1914) his increasing admiration for the scientific method caused Lippmann to recommend that all men's goals be subjected to rigorous rational analysis. Dreams or myths must be dragged out into the light of day. Their sources must be revealed, they must be compared with facts, they must be transformed into actual possibilities. No longer was Lippmann willing to grant that the illusory quality of a myth was irrelevant to its function. Men must have the hard facts with which to operate.

In *Public Opinion* (1922) Lippmann included a largely destructive critique of myths and symbols as factors helping to create delusive mental stereotypes in the public mind. Men respond, he observed, as powerfully to fictions as they do to realities. Mythical symbols such as "Americanism, Progressivism, Law and Order, Justice, Humanity" do not represent specific, logical ideas but rather a "sort of truce or junction between ideas." He did not argue that all myths are entirely false and misleading. In fact, if a myth has affected human conduct for a considerable period of time, it probably contains some truth. "What a myth never contains is the critical power to separate its truths from its errors. For that power comes from realizing that no human opinion, whatever its supposed origin, is too exalted for the test of evidence, that

[42] *Ibid.*, 231.

every opinion is only somebody's opinion." [43] Lippmann advocated the testing of myth through factual observation, realizing full well that such testing not only destroys the value of a myth but the very definition itself. Since his understanding of ideal man was so heavily weighted in the direction of scientific rationality, the destruction of myths—all myths—was not a matter for regret. He was prepared to discard the whole concept in the interest of scientific progress.

The subject of myth appears to have dropped out of Lippmann's thought during the late twenties and early thirties. Only when he came to write from the fresh perspective of *The Good Society* in 1937 did he take up the matter again. Significantly, he returned to Sorel, using the concept of a "social myth" or "vital lie" to explain the stance assumed by the pioneer European liberals of the seventeenth and eighteenth centuries. These thinkers, struggling for individual liberty against state and king and for order in the midst of social turmoil, demanded and received legal recognition of their rights. They then "convinced themselves that the legal rights enforceable in the courts were in essence superhuman. They taught that the laws merely declared inalienable and, therefore, unalterable rights with which men had been endowed by their Creator. . . ." This identification of custom and current judicial decision with "the Laws of Nature and of Nature's God" was the "great myth" by which a new social order was made possible. But the myth quickly served its purpose, and the transmission of it to the nineteenth century encouraged the stultification of laissez-faire capitalism. Nevertheless, argued Lippmann, we must not discredit myth as such. "We must not deny the prophet because he speaks in parables and ephemeral myths." [44] However illusory in substance, myth may still contain profound insight into the realities of existence. Lippmann was now willing to restore myth to something like the place of importance given it by Sorel.

[43] *Public Opinion*, 206, 123.
[44] *The Good Society*, 243, 359.

In the same way that Sorel's impact on Lippmann's early thought has been largely ignored, so also has the later influence of the Cambridge Platonists. Weary of the incessant religious polemics of seventeenth century England, that remarkable group of Puritan ministers—men such as Ralph Cudworth, Henry More, and John Smith—had set out to change the whole focus of the discussion. In so doing, they showed themselves to be a century or more ahead of their time. Ignoring the sore points of doctrinal conflict, they sought for a basic level of agreement, a common core of belief around which the entire religious community could unite. To do this, they felt it necessary to change the linguistic currency, and they seized upon the terminology of Platonism and Neo-Platonism as fitted for their purposes. "The language of Platonism at that time commanded assent with an authority second only to that of Scripture, and to use it in religious exhortation, therefore, was the happiest available method of implying, without aggressively proclaiming, that there were other ways of faith besides those laid down in the current formulae." [45]

Among the Cambridge Platonists, John Smith appears to have been especially interesting to Lippmann. Smith's major contribution involved his insistence on the constant substitution of an *entelechy*, an idea, or a state of mind for the pictorial and dramatic representations of the traditional Christian scheme of doctrine. In effect, he proposed to pierce religious myths to their depths in order to discern the core of universal truth within them—truth which could be expressed as well or better by intellectual abstractions. He saw myth as an allegorized expression of spiritual reality. Lippmann cites Smith's treatment of the myth of the devil as a prime example of his approach. "The devil could mean either 'some apostate spirit as one particular being,' and also 'the spirit of apostasie which is lodged in all men's natures.'" [46] To move from mythical terminology to abstract and philosophized speech is one

[45] Basil Willey, *The Seventeenth Century Background* (New York, 1934), 140. For an excellent account of the work of the Cambridge Platonists, see chap. VIII, 139–73.
[46] *The Public Philosophy*, 131.

way to use "the language of accommodation," thus allowing for a plural interpretation. Those who cannot believe in a personal devil can still accept religious language as referring to the more abstract truth of evil and wickedness in the world. Smith contended, and Lippmann agrees, that this kind of approach is both legitimate and justified: "Truth is content, when it comes into the world, to wear our mantles, to learn our language, to conform itself, as it were, to our dress and fashions: . . . it speaks with the most idiotical sort of men in the most idiotical way, and becomes all things to all men, as every son of truth should do, for their good." [47]

How does Lippmann apply Smith's ideas to his own system? He sees the Cambridge Platonists as seeking to find a way to preserve the essential operating consensus of a community. This, in magnified form, thinks Lippmann, is precisely the problem which is distressing Western culture today. When Smith preached about the devil, he was not addressing his remarks to the religious fundamentalists; "he was addressing men who were unable to believe in the personified devil and yet were still in essential communion with the fundamentalists." Today's political problem in the democracies is somehow to communicate the core of truth embodied in the Western religious heritage to modern men who cannot accept the traditional language but can be addressed in a language of accommodation. As Lippmann evaluated the effort of the Platonists, he wrote: "In this accommodation the Christian Platonists gave up trying to believe what they could not believe. They went on believing that which in essence their fundamentalist neighbors believed. Thus, they could continue to live in the same community with them." [48]

What is the relevance of religious faith to man's existential problems in political society today? It is plain that, for Lippmann, the pictorial and concrete representations involved in the Christian

[47] John Smith, "Of Prophecy," in *Select Discourses*, Rev. Henry Griffin Williams (4th ed., Cambridge, 1859), 173–74. In *The Public Philosophy* Lippmann mistakenly identifies the quotation as having come from Smith's sermon entitled "A Christian's Conflicts and Conquests." See *The Public Philosophy*, 132.

[48] *The Public Philosophy*, 132.

Gospel must be classified as myth. It is true that he is impressed with Paul Tillich's argument that, for almost all men, the abstract must be concretized if it is to be comprehensible. In order for men to be concerned with and committed to transcendent reality, they must believe; in order to believe, men must be confronted by the transcendent in a condescension to man's capacity. There is needed "a being to being relationship, . . . a concrete God, a God with whom man can deal" in his religious experience.[49] Here, however, Lippmann stops. He does not go on with Tillich to consider the possibility and the claim of the Christian faith that God has actually become concretely personal in the man Jesus of Nazareth. Instead, he shifts from the reasoning of Tillich, who, he says, "is a theologian examining the meaning of God," to what he takes to be another style of the problem: "How can men be concerned effectively with ideas and ideals that transcend their personal experience and cannot be verified empirically in the realm of existence?" [50]

Lippmann concedes the importance of the expression of truth in what he earlier referred to as the "Great Scenario"—"an historic drama . . . enacted in Palestine nineteen hundred years ago during the reign of Emperor Tiberius," [51] but he grants this importance primarily in terms of its allegorized and symbolic representation of the nature of ultimate reality. For an increasing number of modern men, he believes, this reality must be spoken of in a language of accommodation, one which moves away from the frame of historical reference. Yet, aware of the power of myth and tradition, Western man cannot afford to emasculate his heritage by depriving it of the strength of the Christian Gospel. While it is the theologian's task to verbalize and systematize truth in terms of the mythical religious drama, it is the philosopher's task to elucidate the structure of reality in a language of accommodation comprehensible to the modern *homo non religiosis*. If both do their

[49] Paul Tillich, *Systematic Theology* (Chicago, 1951–63), I, 211. Cited in *The Public Philosophy*, 126.
[50] *The Public Philosophy*, 127.
[51] *A Preface to Morals*, 32.

jobs, the necessary public consensus of democratic society may be preserved.

Though it cannot be denied that the discussion of these matters in *The Public Philosophy* moves in a distinctly different atmosphere from that of *A Preface to Morals,* some lines of connection between the two volumes remain clear. In the earlier work Lippmann stated that the weakness of religious modernism—the kind of thought represented by Fosdick, for instance—was that it abandons the historic facts of the Christian Gospel, attempting to preserve certain selected, universalized parts of the religious experience. But, said Lippmann, this is to amputate the arm of Christianity's effectiveness: "The fundamentalist goes to the very heart of the matter, therefore, when he insists that you have destroyed the popular foundations of religion if you make your gospel a symbolic record of experience, and reject it as an actual record of events." [52] Thus, in 1929, Lippmann saw the Christian as caught in an impossible dilemma. The faith was acceptable only to that rapidly diminishing number of men who could still believe in its literal historical veracity. Those who recognized that the historicity of the Christian story was no longer supportable and still tried to preserve in some way its universal insights found that, in the process, they destroyed much of the Gospel's ability to command man's allegiance. Religion, as such, had lost its value. A viable substitute had to be discovered.

Today, Lippmann has altered this argument in several important ways. He no longer insists that the acceptance of the Christian Gospel rests solely on some rigid conviction of its historical credibility. Instead, he is willing to grant that the Christian faith is a valuable means of stating and conveying intimations of ultimate truth. Men can receive it in varying ways, depending on their individual intellectual and emotional makeup. They can embrace it on literal terms, as the orthodox supernaturalist does. Or they can see the Gospel story as primarily pictorial imagery or myth and pierce through it to the universal truth about man and his world embodied in it. Though Lippmann himself does not acknowledge

[52] *Ibid.,* 33.

the facticity of the Gospel, he does not now look upon this question as crucial. He does accept what he conceives to be the universal, abstract truths about essence and existence which are "acted out" in the Christian faith. Such an understanding is intimately linked with his rethinking of the meaning and importance of myth.

It is not to be concluded from this analysis that the Lippmann of today regards religious myth from the perspective of someone like Ludwig Feuerbach, the nineteenth century German theologian, whose thought has been influential in the genesis of much modern philosophy. Feuerbach saw theological concepts primarily as projections of man's self-awareness and desire; God was ideal man enlarged on a cosmic screen. In no sense does Lippmann want to assume this stance. Indeed, he sees as a crisis of our time the derangements brought about by the pretensions of finite men whose introverted musings lead them to confuse the self and God.[53] The community consensus of Western society is menaced most fearsomely by those who declare "the death of God." [54] These men reject any concept of an ultimate reality outside man's self. They leave no appeal from the moral dictatorship of the ego.

It is this loss of distinction between public and private worlds which Lippmann conceives to be the great denial of the philosophy of freedom. Within that philosophy, gradually uncovered

[53] See Lippmann, "The Living Organism of Our Society," Vital Speeches of the Day, II (1935), 188: "To know this, to realize the ultimate limitations of government, and to abide by them, is to have that necessary humility which . . . is . . . the beginning of wisdom. Without it men will use political power for ends that government cannot realize, and in the vanity of their delusions fall into all manner of cruelty, disorder, and waste. They will have forgotten to respect the nature of living things, and in their ambition to be as gods among men they will affront the living god. They will not have learned that those who would be more than human end by being less than human." This is a remarkable statement, written twenty years before The Public Philosophy.

[54] Obviously, Lippmann does not use this term in the sense in which it has recently come to be employed in theology; i.e., to designate the specific thought of men like Thomas J. J. Altizer and William Hamilton. Rather, he groups here all those thinkers, both secular and theological, who disregard or deny the relevance or existence of a "public world," standing over against men's private egos.

through the centuries, man is affirmed as free but as also responsible in his freedom to the unchangeable moral patterns of spiritual reality. "If what is good, what is right, what is true, is only what the individual 'chooses' to 'invent,' then we are outside the traditions of civility. We are back in the war of all men against all men. There is left no ground for accommodation among the varieties of men; nor is there in this proclamation of anarchy a will to find an accommodation." [55]

As Lippmann views it, the final and fatal sickness of Western culture is upon us when sizable groups of men are forced by the pressure of modern currents of thought to abandon even their formal adherence to that public philosophy which has sustained our democratic freedom. Once the community is irrevocably split between those who acknowledge a law independent of their own wills and those who do not, between those who recognize the existence of a public world and those who do not, then the foundations for democracy will have disappeared. In times of crisis and strain, democratic methods of legal procedure will be unable to defend themselves against the attacks of arbitrary tyranny. The friends of freedom, therefore, are those who in some way proclaim this public world, a world mythologically symbolized by the Christian drama of God and his creative act. The enemies of freedom, no matter how loudly they may protest their devotion to liberty, are those who preach God's funeral sermon. To undergird and revitalize the public philosophy—the traditions of civility—is the most urgent task of Western man.

[55] *The Public Philosophy*, 134–35.

Though with great difficulty I am got hither, yet
now I do not repent me of all the troubles I have
been at to arrive at where I am. My sword I give to
him that shall succeed me in my pilgrimage, and my
courage and skill to him that can get it. My marks
and scars I carry with me, to be witness for me, that
I have fought his battles who now will be my
rewarder.

Valiant-for-Truth in Bunyan's *Pilgrim's Progress,*
cited by Walter Lippmann in his last editorial
for the New York *World*

Chapter VI

The Public Philosophy

The exploration of Walter Lippmann's understanding of man has
produced two major conclusions. The first is that he has operated
throughout his career with a *person-centered* value system. Always,
he has begun with the proposition that man's nature and needs
are and ought to be the primary objects of political concern. Accepted unquestioningly in the beginning, this basic assumption
took on philosophical flesh and blood in the rational humanism of
A Preface to Morals. In later years it has been spelled out even
more specifically, especially in the serious attempt to discover its
meaningful substantiation. In time Lippmann has come to rest
his case for human worth on the conviction that each man possesses a final, irreducible essence—an "immortal soul"; thus, he is
an "inviolate person." He is convinced that any political system
ignoring this conviction is out of tune with the harmony of ultimate reality.

The second major conclusion is that Lippmann's unfolding pattern of insight into man's value has been accompanied by an increasingly sophisticated understanding of human nature. The
rather superficial picture of irrational man dominating the earliest

148

writings rapidly gave way to that of the rational, disinterested, autonomous individual of the twenties. Under the influence of both external events and internal reflection this conception of human essence was in turn modified and expanded until, today, Lippmann sees man in a much more complex light. He is an individual, discrete and intelligent, but he is also caught up in community. A free creature, his autonomy is yet severely limited by his creaturehood. A being with deep roots in the irrational processes of nature, he is also uniquely involved in the realm of the spirit. In accordance with this view of man the political problem becomes a challenge to the attainment of the maximum personal freedom consistent with the realities of community. This delicate balance can be attained, Lippmann now believes, only through the free recognition of some law higher than human constructs as a final center of authority and judgment.

Within this context, it has been pointed out, the conception of law has progressively taken on new dimensions. Positive law's distinctive characteristic was identified, not as simple coercion, nor as the proper exercise of sovereignty, nor as its correspondence to accepted patterns of procedure, but as *content* shaped and judged by a higher law. Human law ideally evolves in the tension of two realms as men seek to preserve and insure the spiritual value of the person within the limiting contingencies of history. In this process, once that which is the initial dictate of the higher law—the prime value of personhood—has been accepted, certain generalized political maxims emerge. Such basic norms as legal equality and non-arbitrary adjudication are justified, not by pragmatic procedural superiority, but as reasonable inferences from the concept of personhood. Political society is constrained by the higher law to be that kind of society in which each person in community has the opportunity to reach his greatest human potential. The techniques of constitutional democracy—as distinguished from those of "pure" democracy—contribute to the attainment of such a goal (at least within the American context of Lippmann's concern) and are validated by this fact. On the other hand, the rule of a transient, unrestrained majority is seen as a transgression of personhood. Decisions reached in such a process tend to disregard the guiding value. Only political decisions arrived at deliberately and constitutionally—that is, within the limits of the higher law—can stand the test of that law's judgment.

Lippmann's search for a philosophical justification of human worth in higher law has resulted in the radical readjustment of his stance toward religion. He has concluded that the considerations stipulating the value of the person have been gradually, and against great odds, uncovered in the mainstream of the Western intellectual and spiritual tradition. He has also reached the conviction that the clearest, most effective historical witness to this law has been borne by the Christian churches. Western society cannot function as a free and humane community apart from the active recognition and moral acceptance of the "traditions of civility," a public philosophy undergirded by the recognition of spiritual absolutes. For some men the testimony of the Christian Gospel, concretizing the abstractions of universal truth in the communicable framework of the faith, is essential. For others, who can no longer literally accept the Hebraic-Christian drama in any factual sense— and Lippmann thinks this group is now in the great majority— the concepts of faith are not to be discarded but rather must be translated into an acceptable "language of accommodation." The translation's purpose is the accurate preservation and transmission of the universals allegorically embedded in the religious myth.

Such convictions supply the context and, to some extent, the body of Lippmann's most important theoretical work, *The Public Philosophy*. This brief volume does not pretend to be a work distinguished by strikingly original thought.[1] What is attempted is a diagnosis, cogent and understandable, of the basic malady of democratic society and the suggestion, in broad rather than specific terms, of a solution. As such, it represents, perhaps better than any

[1] Cf. Edward Engberg, "Walter Lippmann's World," *Commonweal*, LXXV (1961), 170. This is an important article. It deals with Lippmann's contemporary thought; after reading it, Lippmann wrote to Engberg: "I thank you for the best gift anyone can give an author, which is to understand him." (Walter Lippmann to Edward Engberg, November 7, 1961, in the Lippmann Collection, Sterling Library, Yale University.)

other single document, what might be termed "the mature Lipp-mann." With the principle features of Lippmann's intellectual and philosophical development in mind, it is important to summarize *The Public Philosophy* and its major emphases.

The Mature Lippmann

Lippmann begins *The Public Philosophy* with a discussion of the political manifestations of a contemporary democratic crisis. He sees the history of Western society since World War I as drastic evidence of political decay. Possessing the greatest accumulation of technological power and potential the world has ever known, victorious in battle over all enemies, committed to high ideals and noble purposes, the democratic nations have still failed to achieve the kind of society expected by their people and demanded by the times. Lippmann wrote, "The more I have brooded upon the events which I have lived through myself, the more astounding and significant does it seem that the decline of the power and influence and self-confidence of the Western democracies has been so steep and so sudden. We have fallen far in a short span of time." [2]

The trend which Lippmann describes has become even more pronounced in the years since. American dismay and frustration concerning its purposes and motives—acutely focused in the Viet-nam tragedy—are reflected in both internal schism and external loss of prestige. The problem of how and why this decline has come about are the controversial questions to which Lippmann addresses himself. He traces the political aspects of the process to a "derangement of powers," caused chiefly by the increasing influ-ence of a radical and perverted democratic theory: the sancti-fying of the general will as expressed in the absolute rule of a transient majority. The attempt of "the people" to carry out the complex tasks of government through elected representatives conceived as mere "mouthpieces" of their constituencies has dem-onstrated again and again its inherent impracticability. The omni-competent citizen is a delusion. To trust the subtle, involved intrica-

[2] *The Public Philosophy*, 19–20.

cies of governmental policy administration to a mob is the prelude to political disaster. To make the popular will the final arbiter of truth is to rip the fabric of community and order. Most citizens, Lippmann contends, are or can become competent to consent to or reject broad, general policies; they are competent to elect officials in whose ability, character, and wisdom they have confidence; they can intervene decisively in government whenever there is major crisis or disagreement; in these ways they can insure that the government is vitally responsible to the public. But the effort to administer government *in toto* by public opinion leads inevitably to misgovernment and disorder—a disorder which powerfully tempts men to accept various levels of authoritarianism as the price of order and security. More recently, Lippmann has argued vis-a-vis the policies of President Lyndon Johnson that the abortive attempt to determine policy by popular consensus represents an extension of the same political perversion. Government by consensus may rapidly degenerate into the artificial manipulation of that consensus.

The modern totalitarian counterrevolutions have their roots in this derangement of powers, and specifically in the Jacobin perversion of democracy which emerged in the French Revolution. Instead of gradual reform accomplished within a structure of constitutional, limited government, the Jacobin theory proposes the violent overthrow and destruction of the governing class. The revolution itself is seen as a healing act by which the ills of society supposedly disappear, and the masses—by definition, those who are not a part of the governing power at the time of the revolution —are assumed to have an innate capacity, even a special genius, for governing. With the success of the revolution, however, the post-revolutionary man, enfranchized and emancipated, actually turns out to be, not the New Man, but the old Adam.[3] In this situation the mystical, infallible will of the people is expressed concretely through the total surrender of power to a ruling elite, who themselves artificially create the mass public opinion which is the practical foundation of their rule. Constituting themselves as

[3] See *ibid.*, 61.

revolutionary instruments, the elite exercise increasingly arbitrary and unlimited authority in order to achieve the revolutionary end —the establishment of a particular brand of Utopia on earth. Of course, the citizens of the new order must fit the prescribed pattern and, since the revolution itself has failed to accomplish completely the desired transformation, more drastic and effective modes of human manipulation must be employed. The New Man must be coerced into being.[4]

The Jacobins and their successors made a political religion founded upon the reversal of civility. Instead of ruling the elemental impulses, they stimulated and armed them. Instead of treating the pretension to being a god as the mortal sin original, they proclaimed it to be the glory and destiny of man. . . . Lenin, Hitler, and Stalin, the hard totalitarian Jacobins of the twentieth century, carried this movement and the logical implications of the gospel further and further toward the bitter end.

And what is that bitter end? It is an everlasting war with the human condition: war with the finitude of man and with the moral ends of finite men, and, therefore, war against freedom, against justice, against the laws and against the order of the good society . . . .[5]

It was to prevent such disastrous results that the founders of the American political system, thinks Lippmann, wisely devoted their attention. Though they, like the French, worked in the atmosphere of revolution, most of them suffered no illusions about any infallible general will. The powers of the state were, therefore, divided and balanced so as to insure the people their right to a government by meaningful consent—of and by the people—but, at the same time, to prevent the majority will from exercising despotic, precipitate control. The separation of powers contributes markedly to the state's proper functioning, since the executive is thereby charged with those tasks which cannot be efficiently performed by any other branch. In this regard Lippmann is convinced that the history of the twentieth century demonstrates a dangerous deteriora-

[4] For a full and frightening discussion of this aspect of the totalitarian revolution, see Hannah Arendt, *The Origins of Totalitarianism* (New York, 1961), esp. 437–59.
[5] *The Public Philosophy*, 71.

tion of executive responsibility in American politics, as the legis-
lative body, as an instrument of mass public opinion, usurps powers
which neither rightly nor functionally belong to it. In such areas
as foreign and fiscal policy, for instance, public opinion is increasingly asked to do that which it is not and cannot become qualified
to do.

Lippmann would certainly admit that his reading of recent history and the resulting assessment of the malfunction of democratic government are particular professional judgments, legitimately open to challenge and rational debate. His whole career
demonstrates that he welcomes this type of discussion. But, he is
not—in *The Public Philosophy*—primarily concerned with technical problems of political function. He does not hold the widespread contemporary faith that the basic problems of men can be
solved by tinkering with political machinery. Instead he employs
the political malfunction as a clue to a much more profound
malady—a sickness of Western men's souls. To refurbish or ma-
nipulate political techniques will not cure this sickness. Political
pains are the symptoms of a deep moral infection, a derangement
of being itself. What is urgently required is not the skill of a social
engineer but the wisdom of a moral physician who is concerned
with healing man.[6]

What is the source of the twentieth century man's illness? From
Lippmann's viewpoint, the malady arises, as we have seen, out of
the failure to recognize a reality to which both man's personal experience and the cumulative wisdom of his culture testify: that a
human being is a unique element in reality's total structure, a person who, by virtue of his creation as a rational and self-conscious
being, is aware of his participation in two realms, that of existence
and that of essence.[7] Unhappily, many modern men have been

---

[6] Cf. a statement made by Lippmann as early as 1935, found on page
188 of "The Living Organism of Our Society." "My thesis is that statesmen had better think of themselves as physicians who assist society than
as engineers who plan and fabricate it."

[7] That the concept of the two realms is the indispensable key to an
interpretation of *The Public Philosophy* is supported by a statement made
by Lippmann in reference to Arthur Schlesinger, Jr.'s essay in *Walter Lipp-*

deprived of their ability to comprehend and to relate to the spiritual realm. They have been "brain-washed" to believe only in that which can be sensibly experienced and mathematically verified. Discrediting the witness of the long human struggle for civilization, today's man is cut off from his past, thereby losing touch with the truth which teaches the necessity for the subjugation of man's first nature—existence in self-centered barbarism—by his second, civilized nature.

Medieval man is commonly indicted for his naive, three-storied universe—heaven, earth, and hell—but a strikingly more deficient view of reality is furnished by modern man's conviction that he lives only on one level. In this flat dimension it is impossible to find any final law other than that of his own finite, limited existence. Driven by the ego-centered thrust of his undisciplined nature to demand unlimited freedom for the fulfillment of all desire, he discovers too late that he has actually placed himself under the arbitrary and unpredictable dictatorship of self. The freedom for which he has striven is revealed as a pseudo-freedom producing anxiety, fear, guilt, meaninglessness, and despair. From such false freedom men are impelled to flee. Thus, their demand for total liberty is transformed into a prologue to slavery. Man is by nature unable to exist in a moral vacuum. Having discarded the "public, general, objective, criteria of the true and the false, the right and the wrong," men are defenseless against the onrush of imitation (or, in Paul Tillich's term, "heteronomous") absolutes. The irrational standards of blood, race, nation, and might consume the soul, and men degenerate into the faceless mass so characteristic of the twentieth century.

Man's empirical two-dimensional nature dictates that he cannot be content with the ambiguities and frustrations of the realm of existence. In every human being there is a persistent dream of salvation and perfection. Is this dream evil? Lippmann does not

_____

mann and His Times: "I think he has not wholly understood or sympathized with—no doubt the fault is mine—where . . . [my] search ended in Part II of The Public Philosophy, particularly Chapter 10" (Lippmann to Edward Engberg, November 7, 1961). Chapter 10 sets out the doctrine of the two realms. See The Public Philosophy, 109–22.

think so. Rather, it is the intimation and testimony of a sphere which lies beyond the material horizon. But the dream does raise a crucial question: "Are men then doomed by the very nature of things to be denied the highest good if it cannot be materialized in this world and if, as so large a number of men assume, it will not be materialized in another world?" [8]

In Lippmann's opinion two alternative answers to the question offer themselves. One is the "radical error of the modern democratic gospel" which promises the achievement of heaven's perfect life here on earth. In what Eric Voegelin has analyzed as "modern gnosticism," [9] this secularized version of the Kingdom of God holds out the goal of a redeemed society of transformed men as an historical possibility. The final extension of such a doctrine, as we have seen, is the demonic kingdom of the totalitarians. The contrasting alternative is that to which Lippmann pins his own hopes. It is that human beings may come to recognize that perfection and salvation are possibilities within the nonmaterial sphere of the spirit; they are impossibilities within the context of nature and history. To confuse the two realms is both to inhibit the good life of this world and to falsify the essential life of the spirit.

In actuality Lippmann is not a metaphysician in any important sense of the term. Confining himself largely to a consideration of man's mundane problems, his prime concern is for the confusion arising out of an attempted easy application of ethical absolutes to contingent circumstances. It is here, perhaps, that Lippmann has been most widely misunderstood. He has been accused (by Reinhold Niebuhr, for instance) of advocating a static concept of moral reality, resulting logically in a fossilized brand of political casuistry similar to that of the Middle Ages.[10] On the contrary,

[8] *The Public Philosophy*, 109.

[9] See Eric Voegelin, *The New Science of Politics* (Chicago, 1952), 107–91.

[10] Cf. Reinhold Niebuhr, "The Democratic Elite and American Foreign Policy," in *Walter Lippmann and His Times*, 170: "His [Lippmann's] moral answer is the restitution of 'natural-law' norms. Traditional conceptions of natural law presuppose a classical ontology which equates history with nature and does not allow for the endless contingencies of history and the variety of its configurations."

however, Lippmann has specifically asserted that in the practical area there are no such hard and fast rules. The virtues of existence apply to beings who, in the words of the Apostle Paul, "are still under the law," [11] subject to the unpredictable limitations of history and the indeterminate dimensions of human freedom. For such men, words like "liberty," "equality," "fraternity," and "justice" are shaped in their concrete interpretations by the dynamic flux of circumstance. To apply absolute virtues to the actual world men must employ Aristotle's virtue of prudence, keeping in mind the philosopher's advice: "Matters concerned with conduct and what is good for us have no fixity . . . [and] the agents themselves must in each case consider what is appropriate to the occasion." [12] Men must seek "the mean" which stands at that point in experience where the good is most effectively preserved *under the circumstances*. While Lippmann does not believe, realistically, that all men are equally capable of such effective use of prudence, still his prescription for the spiritually aware is not in any sense a universalized and rigorous "rule book" morality. The public philosophy cannot be equated with complicated legalism. Indictments of his thought on this basis prove only that many modern thinkers become irrationally defensive when anything smacking of natural law concepts is advanced.

Within the realm of existence men cannot expect to find moral perfection or absolute certainty. Even that central necessity for the realization of personhood—human freedom—is, under the conditions of worldly life, fluid and ambiguous. Men must constantly be open to new dimensions of freedom in the everchanging pattern of experience. There is neither static nor unlimited freedom.

It is exactly to this human condition—one of ambiguous freedom, partial determinability, contingency, and variability—that the traditions of civility are addressed. "The worldly wisdom of the good life" [13] is historically evolved, and it does not apply to the

[11] I Timothy 1:9–10. Cited in *The Public Philosophy*, 110.

[12] Aristotle, *Nichomachean Ethics*, Book II, ch. ii, 1104a. Cited in *The Public Philosophy*, 112.

[13] *The Public Philosophy*, 112

realm of essence but to the actual world of diversity and change. Men's political knowledge, for example, is the cumulative result of both experience and thought in the down-to-earth, practical task of constructing governments for earthly kingdoms, not heavenly ones.

But the question remains: what relationship, if any, exists between the working maxims of the good life, and the absolute virtues of the spirit? In criticizing Lippmann's thought, Reinhold Niebuhr has argued that if men do full justice to the contingencies of history, ". . . our norms are bound to be no more precise than the general feeling that there are standards of justice which transcend any conceivable positive law." [14] Yet, as Paul Ramsey and others have convincingly demonstrated, Niebuhr's own thought does not remain consistent with this lean definition of the function and content of moral norms.[15] Lippmann would certainly react negatively to such disparagement. True, men must prudently choose a largely unpredictable course of action in the context of every particular situation. But—and this is of fundamental importance—"the agents . . . do not improvise a rule which they consider appropriate to the occasion. They 'consider' something. And that something, says Aristotle, is that 'it is the nature of things'—including the nature of the worldly virtues—'to be destroyed by defect and excess.' " [16] No ethical choice is an isolated one. Contextual ethical decision amid the contingencies of history is a slippery and futile exercise without some overarching background of stable and limiting value. It is navigation without sextant or compass.

Lippmann does not argue that the absolute principles of the spiritual realm can be neatly transported into the sphere of existence. There are no easy, precise solutions to intricate, puzzling problems of ethical action. "The deposit of wisdom in the Bible and in the classic books does not contain a systematic and comprehensive statement of moral principles from which it is possible

[14] Niebuhr, "The Democratic Elite and American Foreign Policy," 170.
[15] See Paul Ramsey, *Nine Modern Moralists* (Englewood Cliffs, N.J., 1962), 111–47.
[16] *The Public Philosophy*, 112.

to deduce with clarity and certainty specific answers to concrete questions." If man possessed an encyclopedia of all that the prophets and the philosophers have taught, he still would not know "how to make laws, how to govern a state, how to educate his children—how, in fact, to decide the problems that the priest encounters in the confessional, the doctor with his patients, the lawyer with his clients, the judge with his litigants, the man of affairs in his business." [17] As Lippmann comprehends it, the higher law does not operate so as to lift the burden of moral choice and responsibility from individual man. To do so would deprive man of the root of his personhood, thus contradicting the essence of the higher law itself.

Both man's moral responsibility and his inner moral conflict arise out of his consciousness of the two worlds in which he lives and of the two allegiances he owes. The more he emerges from the primordial human condition in which mere custom "is the principle magistrate of his life," the more aware he becomes that he is drawn between two disparate realms of being and can give total loyalty to neither. In these circumstances the wisdom of his heritage—the tradition of civility—instructs him that the two realms are inseparable but distinct, "that man must work out his destiny in the balance, which is never finally fixed between them." The two spheres cannot be united; they cannot be dissociated. "They must be related by striking, maintaining, redressing a balance between them." The final word comes from neither of the two spheres, for within the realm of existence truth speaks no final word. There are only "the provisional points of equilibrium of an unending tension among variable elements." [18] Where the point of equilibrium will be in any particular context is never determinable a priori. It must be empirically judged, but always within the broad principles of the public philosophy. These fixed values of the realm of essence can never be fully systematized; neither can they be ignored.

Toward the close of *The Public Philosophy* Lippmann summa-

[17] *Ibid.*, 113.
[18] *Ibid.*, 117–19.

rizes the political theses derived from this understanding of man and reality. He asserts that free, liberal institutions were conceived and established by men who believed in a particular kind of public philosophy: "Though there have been many schools in this philosophy, there are fundamental principles common to all of them: that, in Cicero's words, 'law is the bond of civil society,' and that all men, governors and the governed, are always under, are never above laws . . . and that the highest laws are those upon which all rational men of good will, when fully informed, will tend to agree." [19] Liberal democracy and political freedom make no sense when separated from these higher laws. In fact, democracy cannot, in the long run, be made to function except by men who possess and adhere to the public philosophy which gave such a form of political organization birth.

Lippmann is convinced that the essential content of the public philosophy has been progressively discovered by men intelligently aware of the two-dimensional quality of reality. These men stand preeminently in a long natural law tradition stretching from the Stoics and the Roman lawyers through the Christian fathers and Thomas Aquinas.[20] After the Renaissance and the Reformation this tradition, newly formulated by men like Richard Hooker and John Locke, supplied the philosophy of the English Revolution of 1668 and the American Revolution of 1776.[21]

The genius of the English and American political systems is that in their provisions the precepts of the public philosophy

[19] *Ibid.*, 123.

[20] See *ibid.*, 81–84. For historical background on the development of the natural law tradition, Lippmann relies heavily on Ernest Barker, *Traditions of Civility* (Cambridge, 1948) and Otto Gierke, *Natural Law and the Theory of Society*, trans. Ernest Barker. (Boston, 1957).

[21] Cf. John Courtney Murray, *We Hold These Truths* (New York, 1960), 14: "the American Proposition rests on the more traditional conviction that there are truths; that they can be known; that they must be held; for if they are not held, assented to, consented to, worked into the texture of institutions, there can be no hope of founding a true City, in which men may dwell in dignity, peace, unity, justice, well-being, freedom." For a challenge to Lippmann's view, see Sidney Hook, "Do the People Rule and Can They?" *New York Times Book Review*, (July 14, 1963), 1ff.

have been made concrete by treating them as contracts. If a contract is viewed as an agreement voluntarily reached, it implies that the parties involved "have thought, felt and judged the matter together." Out of such an agreement can be derived workable criteria for the adjudication of disputes; respective rights and duties can be defined. These are the essential characteristics of a constitutional system—a legal state. The establishment of political relationships by contract is of such importance that in the Western World the making of the contracts of government and of society have usually been regarded as marking—historically and symbolically—the crossing of the line which divides barbarity from civility.[22]

For most of the unwritten laws of the good society there exist no historic documents of contract. Yet, in the public philosophy, it is assumed that such laws are contractual and rest on consent. The principle of contract is preserved in myths (Lippmann uses the giving of the Ten Commandments as an example) which speak of an original covenant entered into by the first ancestors and binding on all descendants. That such myths may constitute historical fiction is not the question: "A fiction is not necessarily a false hood. It may be the vehicle of truth."[23] And the truth is that positive laws do not prevail unless the lawmakers, the judges, the law enforcers, and finally, the people generally, are attached to those laws. Unless behind the fabric of legislation is a large-scale public consent to the basic philosophy of the laws, no free, democratic government can long exist.

If Lippmann is correct in this line of argument, then the public philosophy is inseparable from the full maintenance of freedom within order. Such a philosophy must, however, be reevaluated, rethought, and restated by each generation in its turn. It must also, as a public duty, be effectively preserved and transmitted to the coming generation. Such a conclusion obviously stands in direct contradiction to the widespread modern theory of "privatism," in which what men believe about the ultimate issues of life is alleged

[22] *The Public Philosophy*, 128.
[23] *Ibid.*, 130.

to have no public but only private significance. Lippmann wrote, "The outer defenses of the free way of life stand upon the legal guarantees against the coercion of belief. But the citadel is vacant because the public philosophy is gone, and all that the defenders of freedom have to defend in common is a public neutrality and a public agnosticism." [24] Lippmann feels that not only the future prospects of constitutional government but the nature of democracy demand that Western men face squarely the probable consequences of the loss of a basic philosophical consensus.

Lippmann does not, of course, believe that the public philosophy can be transmitted or renewed by forcing it upon men. The argument that to have a public philosophy of any kind requires some authoritative "Office" to interpret, define, and enforce its provisions,[25] shows a defective understanding of the nature of a democratic consensus. A philosophy which enshrines the integrity of each person as its cardinal tenet cannot by definition be one of coerced belief. Neither is Lippmann hopeful, however, that simple exhortation can accomplish the task. Men today have largely lost the capacity to believe in the invisible, and this capacity can only be restored by a concerted effort on the part of "men of light and leading." Such men must be open-minded enough to take seriously once again the possibility of two dimensions of reality. They must apply their rational powers and spiritual intuition to more than the flat world of positivism.

It must be understood that Lippmann is not calling for educators and philosophers to put on intellectual blinders, committing themselves to a position they cannot sustain with integrity. Rather, he is deploring, as has many another concerned observer, that widespread contemporary intellectual stance which chooses to wash its hands of any serious involvement with ultimate moral questions. Lippmann opposes the popular perversion which re-

24 *Ibid.*, 88.

25 For this contention, see Frankel, *The Democratic Prospect*, 189. Frankel rejects the necessity of a public philosophy but argues that an "office" would be essential to maintain one. He concedes, however, that Lippmann does not propose or want such an "office."

gards the scientific method (of the natural sciences) as being "the only method by which we ever learn anything: by which, that is to say, we make solid additions to the growing heap of definitely established knowledge." [26] Granted that the knowledge of "essence" does not arrive in such neat intellectual building blocks, yet men have continuously sought a working knowledge of the realm of the spirit, discovering insights and values of significant pragmatic importance. To turn our backs upon this history is to amputate a major portion of our own spiritual anatomy, for inescapably we are products of this centuries-old struggle. We are not asked to receive the conclusions of the past as infallible and complete; neither is it logical to disregard them.

Lippmann's confidence in the future rests on his faith that if men once again take seriously the two dimensions of reality, applying their rational powers and spiritual intuition to more than the flat world of positivism, it can be shown to skeptics "that there are certain principles which, when they have been demonstrated, only the willfully irrational can deny, that there are certain obligations binding on all men who are committed to a free society, and that only the willfully subversive can reject them." In this immensely difficult task philosophy and theology are the decisive studies, for "in them are defined the main characteristics of the images of man which will be acted upon in the arts and sciences of the epoch." [27] The responsibility of teachers in schools and universities is not simply to receive and parrot the traditions of the public philosophy but to apply creative intellect so as to devise convincing demonstrations that the principles of the good society are not subjective but objective, not irrational but rational, not private but public. Only such demonstrations can alter the terms of modern discourse, now so prejudicially stacked in favor of positivism, subjectivism, and Jacobin democracy. The arduous nature of the task is matched only by the challenge of the problem.

[26] Morton White, *Social Thought in America: The Revolt Against Formalism* (2nd ed.; Boston, 1957), 82.
[27] See *The Public Philosophy*, 89, 136.

Lippmann and His Critics

Walter Lippmann has chosen to associate the public philosophy with the Western tradition of natural law. In so doing, he has provoked great critical reaction to his position and, for many, raised the most serious doubts. Therefore, it is essential to clarify exactly what the alignment with natural law theory involves for Lippmann and wherein he accepts or rejects the classical content of that tradition.

In this connection an observation by Edward Engberg is perceptive: "Mistrust of Natural Law theory, any natural law theory, runs deep and wide in American political thought. The excesses of divine monarchs, inquisitors and Cotton Mather are visited indiscriminately upon anyone who tries to get a sympathetic hearing for anything smacking of a law of nature." [28] An examination of the attacks on Lippmann's views underscores this statement. Much of the criticism is directed, not against his specific thought, but against the general idea of natural law in any or all of its historical manifestations. It is indicative of the problem with which Lippmann is dealing that so many critics simply refuse to hear him when he propounds a theory classified as natural law.[29] Two cases in point may be cited.

Arthur Schlesinger, Jr., an acute and friendly observer, in a largely laudatory essay on Lippmann moves along easily until he reaches the place where he must deal with the concept of the pub-

[28] Engberg, "Walter Lippmann's World," 169. Cf. also Murray, We Hold These Truths, 17.

[29] For examples of this approach, see Hook, "Do the People Rule and Can They?", 1; Oscar Handlin, "Does the People's Rule Doom Democracy?", Commentary, XX (July, 1955), 13. In a much more sophisticated and meaningful manner Hans J. Morgenthau questions Lippmann from this angle. See "Reason and Restoration in the West," New Republic, CXXXII (Feburary 21, 1955), 12–13ff. Max Ways has commented: "Our plural beliefs are probably capable of enough reconciliation to form a public philosophy, usable for politics. What prevents this is the modern temper, which refuses to let such a discussion be held." See Max Ways, Beyond Survival (New York, 1959), 17.

lic philosophy. This he refuses to take seriously. The idea of natural law is an "artificial construct," avers Schlesinger, and he can only explain Lippmann's "flight from the human problem" [30] as the work of a compensated mind, swinging, like a pendulum, contra-cyclically to the dominating suppositions of the day. He sees Lippmann as having moved from the dynamic pluralism of *The Phantom Public* to a static monism in *The Public Philosophy*. And he finds it comforting to assume that, since 1955, Lippmann has slowly backed away from his adherence to natural law. He draws this conclusion, interestingly enough, from Lippmann's comments on the lack of a common value system between the Western world and the Communists.

Morton White is another example. In the second edition of his book, *Social Thought in America: The Revolt Against Formalism*, Professor White included a specifically written epilogue, entitled "Original Sin, Natural Law, and Politics." The purpose of the additional material was to consider the views of "two of the most distinguished critics of the liberal tradition: Reinhold Niebuhr . . . and Walter Lippmann who, in his most recent work, has bemoaned the disappearance of what he calls 'The Public Philosophy'. . . ." [31] After devoting the first portion of his epilogue to a fairly specific attack on Niebuhr's views, White turns to Lippmann. In contrast, however, his method involves no detailed consideration whatsoever of Lippmann's actual presentation in *The Public Philosophy*; rather, he devotes his entire time to an assault on the traditional natural law position which he understands to have been set forth by Aquinas and John Locke. In so doing he attempts to saddle Lippmann with a good many views and convictions which he has never publicly espoused.

It must be noted that the abundance of this type of criticism is partly due to the fact that Lippmann has failed to deal with his own natural law theory in any truly definitive way. His terse and generalized comments leave substantive questions unanswered. To examine the major arguments advanced against him, while seeking

[30] Schlesinger, "Walter Lippmann: The Intellectual v. Politics," 221.
[31] White, *Social Thought in America*, xi.

in the process to clarify his own position, may be as effective a way as any to delineate his views. For this purpose the writings of two men provide convenient material: first, those of Morton White, just mentioned; and second, the work of David Spitz,[32] who in a brief, clear fashion has summed up many of the most frequently advanced arguments.

Along with many contemporaries, White's principal quarrel with natural law theorists is within the realm of the viable possibility of essences—fixed, unchanging structures of truth and objective reality, having meaning apart from the subjective manipulations of men. White offers the argument that it is extremely difficult to prove the existence of these essences to those who do not believe in them. "A theorist of natural law will frequently have to face people who don't believe that there are self-evident moral principles to begin with. But how does he get the machinery rolling then? Where can he begin?" [33]

Now, before this argument can count for much, it must be made clear exactly what it is that Lippmann is trying to establish when he talks about "essence." In this regard White would have done well to pay more attention to Lippmann's own views, rather than centering his attack on Aquinas and Locke. For Lippmann, the realm of "essence" is that area where objects are present to the mind. He admits that the term "essence" is an ambiguous one, but he finds no other to replace it. What he seems to mean is that in the realm of understanding, man is relatively and distinctively free to seek out and confront the undistorted nature of conceptual absolutes, a confrontation he can never make in the realm of existence. The spiritual nature of man, which includes his freedom partially to transcend the limitations of physical existence in the realm of the mind, enables him to envision and conceive of a

---

[32] In *Patterns of Anti-Democratic Thought* Professor Spitz is highly critical of Lippmann's stricture against unlimited majority rule. See 105–10. In *Democracy and the Challenge of Power* (New York, 1958) Spitz addresses himself specifically to the natural law concepts of *The Public Philosophy*. It is the argument of this latter volume which is summarized here.

[33] White, *Social Thought in America*, 274.

"realm of being where men are redeemed and regenerated and the evils of the world have been outgrown." [34]

Lippmann's approach actually bypasses the tricky and, perhaps, finally unanswerable question as to the objective "reality" of this realm of essence—at least in any sense of a super-world of essences—apart from and beyond the world of existence. What he argues for is a different sort of reality, based on a common sense recognition of the functionality of that ideal or perfected world which rationally underlies all man's awareness of imperfection in the sensible world. The kind of ideals or essences which make up this world, Lippmann believes, are apprehended as the cumulative result of man's long, historic struggle to achieve a rational and coherent understanding of his own total experience. Thus, he waives the question of the actuality of some transcendent or metaphysical quality such as "perfect justice," regarding it as irrelevant. What is relevant and also indisputable is that men, as reasoning beings, have gradually discovered concepts of perfect justice which have both content and significance. These concepts can nowhere be sensibly duplicated *in toto*; nevertheless they lie behind and function as norms for all systems of existential justice.

Can the realm of essence, conceived in this manner, become the meaningful subject of conversation, exploration, and explication among modern men? Or is White correct in assaying such a task as hopeless? Lippmann's answer would seem to be that such essences do not actually require the kind of demonstration which White finds so difficult to accept. They merely need to be designated and clarified. In other words, it is nonsense to attempt to prove to a rational individual that he possesses rationality. And rationality empirically includes the faculty enabling a man to transcend the limitations of surrounding circumstances and to conceive of perfection and fulfillment. Every man who thinks at all discovers himself "living in two worlds and subject to two allegiances. There is the familiar world which he knows through his senses and there is a world of his mind. He is drawn between the two disparate

[34] *The Public Philosophy*, 116.

realms of being, and the tension within them is the inexhaustible theme of human discourse." [35]

Faced with the fact of human experience in these two realms, men then have the problem of evaluating the significance of each realm and of adjusting the tension between them. Of course, it is possible—and Lippmann bemoans the fact that many men choose this path—to resolve the tension by denying that the realm of essence ought to have any relevance to actual life and decision. Men cannot eliminate their encounter with intimations of essence, but they can ignore these encounters and strive to draw all norms out of the realm of "things as they appear to be"—the world of existence. Still, it is difficult, if not impossible, to conceive of any rational man functioning in life-situations, making choices among alternative opinions or actions, without continuously falling back on some structure of imagination which depicts that individual's own "ideal" arrangement of the circumstances. What justification do men have to classify a realm which is both experientially verifiable and pragmatically important as delusive? On what basis, except by arbitrary definition, is the realm of existence counted as more "real" than that of essence?

To argue in this way is not to attempt to substantiate any particular value arrived at within the realm of essence. Rather, it is to dispute the crude positivist stance which insists that the only evidence worth hearing in life is that which can be measured and verified in certain selected scientific ways.

"In the traditions of civility," Lippmann asserts, "the prevailing view has been that the two realms are inseparable but disparate, and that man must work out his destiny in the balance, which is never fixed finally between the two." [36] This appears to be a meaningful way to describe a phase of man's experience in the making of value-judgments. To deny the relevance of the realm of essence in this process is to do two drastic deeds. First, it is to cut oneself off from the past and the accumulated wisdom of his own history (which is the history of the race), thereby falling into the

[35] *Ibid.*, 117.
[36] *Ibid.*

error of some modern empirical philosophy which insists that here is nothing to be learned from the history of philosophy before "the revolution." It is, as Lord Acton noted, a familiar feature of revolutionary zeal to desire to abolish the past and to start again ("No more tradition's chains shall bind us.").

Second, and more seriously, such a denial bifurcates a man, for he is called on to cut away and discard a self-evident portion of his own being. To consign to the ash heap of irrelevance the continued intimations within his own spirit of the realm of truth, beauty, and goodness, unmarred by the imperfections of the mundane world, is to measurably reduce and cripple man's interior experience. Indeed, it is to make one less than a man, in any understandably human sense.

Lippmann believes that men of learning who take the whole man seriously, including the evidence of a realm of essence, can argue convincingly that an awareness of this realm has necessary meaning. His analysis of modern man's predicament is based upon a reasonably hard-bitten consideration of the empirical fate of men and nations who have lost or ignored this awareness.

Critics of this position consistently raise the question: can anything of concrete value arise out of man's intellectual grapplings with the problem of essences? To grant that rational concepts of the perfected nature of things do play a part in man's experience is one thing; to draw out of such awareness concrete guidelines for action is another. Thus, Morton White contends that even if men should be persuaded of the existence of "Lippmann's essences," such things as principles of political morality remain neither self-evident to all men nor logically deducible from the essences.

This same objection is advanced by Professor David Spitz, who upbraids natural law theorists for being unable to prescribe more than the commonplace distinction that there is a vital, necessary difference between the "is" and the "ought" in politics. This is all that natural law can logically declare, insists Professor Spitz, and consequently, its declaration is insignificant.[37]

[37] Spitz, *Democracy and the Challenge of Power*, 120. Cf. also Frank H. Underwood, review of *The Public Philosophy*, in *Canadian Forum*, XXXIV

Two points should be made in response to this contention as it relates to Lippmann. First, there is no intention on Lippmann's part to assert that the concrete guidelines for action arising out of natural law are easily self-evident to all men. They are self-evident to men of "right reason," but men possessed of perfectly functioning right reason belong themselves to the realm of essence; that is, such a man is conceivable to the mind but does not concretely exist. Does this destroy the case? It does not, unless one wants to argue that since there is no *perfect* human reason capable of arriving at total apprehension of truth, *relatively dependable* human reason is useless for arriving at relatively dependable apprehensions. Lippmann does not contend that any thinker or group of thinkers possess "right reason," in a total sense. But he does argue that the cumulative history of many men's rational struggles in the search for truth is important, and that the results of that struggle are relatively dependable. And he does assert that the intellectual history of Western man points to the emergence of certain values which are basic as guidelines to Western man's action. Thus, he would contend that much more than Spitz's simple principle of "oughtness" can be derived from men's continuing attempts to understand the nature of things.

Second, Lippmann argues that even this "commonplace distinction" between "is" and "ought" is vastly important. It is this distinction which declares that a structure of good independent of men's arbitrary choices operates in the decision process, and this, thinks Lippmann, is a basic essential for the good life and the good society. His natural law does contain, as Spitz indicates, the traditional assertion that all rational men know that they ought to do good and avoid evil. Lippmann's special emphasis, however, is on the absolute necessity for a recognition of the existence of a meaningful and relatively knowable "ought." If society ignores the realm of essences as one source of an objective structure of morality, as

---

(March, 1955), 284: "When Mr. Lippmann tries to become concrete about it [natural law] . . . his statements become so generalized that everybody can agree with them because they don't mean anything in particular."

much modern thought counsels, then a continuing public moral consensus of any kind is both highly doubtful and logically accidental. Unrestrained by a sense of objective or universal values, every man is theoretically free to devise his own standards. Political action then stands to degenerate into power contests in which might is finally determinate.[38] Such a world is that of the barbarian, not that of free, responsible persons. It is Hobbes's world of "continual fear," of war by every man against every man, in which man's life is "solitary, poor, brutish, and short." The prime content of natural law is its witness to the fact that, in addition to each individual's private world, there is also a public world which bears upon him.

Growing out of this conviction is a second major proposition which Lippmann conceives as a part of the natural law: the value of the human person. In his view the structure of empirical reality gives evidence that man is a unique type of living being. His argument is the familiar one that man's self-awareness, his ability rationally to transcend himself, and other associated characteristics mark him as unique, as a *person*. Each man's awareness of himself as a person, together with his recognition of this same uniqueness in other human beings, validate a certain spiritual equality among men, at least in the minimum sense of each man's right to be treated as a person by other persons. Out of this natural right arises the whole structure of legal equality. Men are subject to law, but only as persons; that is, their status demands a nonarbitrary system of legal function which makes every possible provision for men to express and protect their personhood. It is Lippmann's

[38] "It [the public philosophy] does, to be sure, affirm an ideal. Everyone possesses, because everyone acts upon, one conception or another of human nature. Hitler had his, and it offended many. Are they to say, therefore, that his was not simply another man's dish of tea; is every opinion on the subject as good as any other? Or does man have recourse to something which enables him to call foul; a guiding principle which will enable man, at the very least, to avoid squandering the products of blood, sweat, and thought laid up by past generations for his benefit?" Engberg, "Walter Lippmann's World," 170.

contention that while no existing political structure can ever be totally approved by the natural law,[39] no system of constitutional democracy can validate itself except in final dependence upon the natural law's proclamation that all men are "inviolable persons."

Those who object to this line of argument have a tendency to contradict themselves in the process. Spitz, for instance, believes that such principles as that of the "inviolable person" are both useless and meaningless when it comes to specific cases. At the same time he dogmatically asserts: "If we wish to maintain democracy, and the democratic process leads to a result incompatible with the natural law teaching, we must deny the natural law guardians the right to prevent that democratic result from coming into being. We must abide by the will of the majority, even if that will is, by natural law standards, wrong." He then quickly adds, by way of footnote: "I do not, of course, imply by this that a democrat cannot properly oppose the will of the majority where that will violates *democratic*, as distinct from natural law, standards."[40]

This involves Spitz—and here he is representative of many liberal democrats—in both an inconsistency and a dilemma. His inconsistency lies in the fact that, by juggling terminology, he rejects natural law while at the same time assigning to democratic procedures exactly the same functional role.[41] His dilemma is that which Lippmann, among others, long ago recognized and for which he has consistently sought a solution: where can a democrat ever find ground from which to oppose a political decision democratically arrived at? By Spitz's definition democracy rests on a "final (because ultimate and inescapable) trust . . . in the wisdom . . . and in the intrinsic sense of decency of a people."[42]

One can hardly resist asking about this "sense of decency"—

---

[39] "*The Public Philosophy* does not claim . . . an ordinance of God for any social order extant or conceivable within known human capacity" Engberg, "Walter Lippmann's World," 170.

[40] Spitz, *Democracy and the Challenge of Power*, 124, 204 (n. 30).

[41] For a fuller consideration of this general type of fallacy in strictures against natural law, see the lucid discussion by A. P. d'Entrèves, *Natural Law* (London, 1951).

[42] Spitz, *Democracy and the Challenge of Power*, 128.

what it is and whence it is acquired. More pertinently, suppose this faith in the people proves to be ungrounded—or, even more to the point, suppose one can trust the people to follow legally sanctioned democratic procedures but cannot trust them not to employ these procedures to abolish the substance of freedom? What then? If the democrat protests such actions merely because he *prefers* individual liberty and respect for personal integrity, he has no case, for the transient majority has freely decided against him. If he argues only for the pragmatic value of free legal processes, he is involved in a complicated contest of results—the outcome of which can only be determined in retrospect and which finally depends on a subjective judgment as to what kind of result is most desired. If he seeks to substantiate his preference for democracy on some more objective basis, falling back on the contention that there are intrinsic values in free government which men should recognize and support, then any full development of his argument moves him extremely close to Lippmann's position.

In this light the argument that the principles derived from natural law are so general and limited as to be inconsequential fails to carry weight. Democratic government, Lippmann points out, is a structure of existence, not essence. As such, it is a system dependent on discussion, persuasion, and compromise. But no meaningful discussion is practical or productive unless issues are joined within a broad context of agreement which gives shape to the discussion. Compromise is a dead technique unless the basic principles being compromised are clearly recognized by the parties involved.[43]

A contemporary example of this truth is the Cold War. Instead of illustrating a move away from the concept of the public philosophy (as Arthur Schlesinger argues)[44] Lippmann's thought in this regard furnishes a working example of its importance. He has analyzed the Cold War conflict so as to show that there are two major worlds of political discourse existent today.[45] These two

[43] For a clarifying discussion of the relationship between compromise and principle in politics, see John H. Hallowell, *The Moral Foundation of Democracy* (Chicago, 1954), 27–47.

[44] Schlesinger, "Walter Lippmann: The Intellectual v. Politics," 221.

[45] See *The Communist World and Ours* (Boston, 1958).

worlds are (or, at least, have been) ethically incommensurate with each other, to a high degree. There is little common language of discussion. Words like "freedom" and "justice" mean one thing to the communist and another to the Western democrat. In such a situation little effective compromise is possible—at least as progress toward an eventual solution. What is possible is described in the familiar term "peaceful coexistence"—a balance of power based on more or less accidental concurrence of national interest. The hope is that this balance will provide time and opportunity for the slow development of a working consensus between the two forces, perhaps partially through the discovery or rediscovery of common values based on "the nature of things."

Another of Spitz's objections to Lippmann's idea of natural law involves the charge that the acceptance of a public philosophy subjects men to intolerable restrictions, limiting their freedom and forcing conformity to arbitrary standards.[46] This same point has been made by Archibald MacLeish, the distinguished poet and dramatist. MacLeish finds it as difficult as Schlesinger and others to understand Lippmann's contemporary thought. For him, the public philosophy represents "a retreat from the idea of freedom as that idea has been understood in this Republic." The legitimate American idea of freedom, contends MacLeish, is "the boundless liberty of the individual human spirit." The irresistible flow of history is toward the increasing individualization of man. "Ever-increasing consciousness which means ever-increasing individuality, is the law of human gravity and cannot be reversed." What Lippmann has mistakenly tried to do is to go backward, back to the outmoded concepts of community under natural law which dominated the ancient and medieval worlds—"a seductive dream in a time like ours—a dream which drags powerfully at the hearts of those who have lost, or those who have not yet learned, the difficult hope of which human freedom is the ultimate expression." Lippmann, so the argument goes, has perverted the American dream of liberty, for he insists that true freedom "was founded on the postulate that there was a universal order on which all reason-

[46] Spitz, *Democracy and the Challenge of Power*, 123–27.

able men were agreed; *within that* public agreement on the fundamentals and on the ultimates, it was safe to permit, and it would be desirable to encourage, dissent and dispute." MacLeish sees such a concept of freedom as a betrayal of real liberty, a contradiction of the whole modern movement of art and culture with its emphasis on the exploration of the autonomous self, "that inward country." [47]

MacLeish, like many other critics, ignores the true significance of Lippmann's two realms. In an answer to MacLeish's article Lippmann points out that MacLeish has loosely employed two inconsistent ideas of freedom. First, he holds that the American concept of freedom is "the boundless liberty of the individual human spirit." But he also speaks of "the modern democratic belief in the greatest *possible* individual freedom." [48] These two definitions can be properly related only if one conceives of reality in terms of both essence and existence. In a one-dimensional world there can obviously be no "boundless" liberty, for one is constantly colliding with the equally valid liberties of others. The hard facts of social existence, if nothing else, dictate inescapable bounds. It is only in the realm of essence—"that inward country"—that one's liberty can truly be boundless; on the plane of history (existence) there are always necessary limits. The wise and desirable limits in this realm are provided by the public philosophy, a core of indispensable reflections of reality, which draws lines around freedom so that it does not become moral anarchy and destroy itself. "If free men do not keep their public actions within the bounds, they will make free government unworkable, and in the ensuing disasters and disorders freedom will be lost." [49]

One final objection to Lippmann's philosophy advanced by Spitz and others is worthy of consideration. Spitz accuses Lippmann of having deserted his own standard of reason by emphasizing the role of belief or faith in the process of adherence to the public philosophy: "The capacity or will to believe is not an ap-

[47] All quotations in this paragraph are from Archibald MacLeish, "The Alternative," *Yale Review*, n. s. XLIV (June, 1955), 486–93.

[48] *Ibid.*, 491, 487.

[49] Lippmann, "A Rejoinder," *Yale Review*, n. s. XLIV (June, 1955), 500.

peal to reason; nor is it a convincing demonstration of the truth of what is believed." [50] Such a contention carries with it the argument that, when men depend on reason alone, there can be no real agreement on the postulates of natural law. And if there is no agreement, it is evident that no such rational structure exists.

Already established is the contention that Lippmann's understanding of the nature of man and reason will not fit the pattern of narrow rationalism. William Barrett, among others, has pointed out the gulf that separates a *rational* man, seen primarily as a thinking machine, and a *reasonable* man, conceived as a total personality—thinking, feeling, believing, willing.[51] In this sense of the word, Lippmann is not a rationalist. Rather, he seeks to be reasonable, and he sees man's perception of the two realms, not as an exercise in logical syllogisms or scientific empiricism, but as an achievement of the whole man. "The concepts and the principles of the public philosophy have their being in the realm of immaterial entities. They cannot be experienced by our sense organs or even, strictly speaking, imagined in visual or tangible terms. Yet these essences, these abstractions, which are out of sight and out of touch, are to have and to hold men's highest loyalties." [52] What Lippmann recognizes is that loyalty is finally a matter of commitment; and though the choice should be and can be a reasonable one, it ultimately involves an act of faith, a venture into the world of "things not seen."

A consideration of these various criticisms has provided a general explication of Lippmann's somewhat distinctive use of the natural law concept. Certain summary statements may be useful.

First, the central content of the natural or higher law is its insistence on a framework of moral value, a public world which is "not someone's fancy, someone's prejudice, someone's wish or rationalization, a psychological experience and no more. It is there

[50] Spitz, *Democracy and the Challenge of Power*, 122. See also the article by Professor Spitz, "Freedom, Virtue, and the New Scholasticism," *Commentary*, XXVIII (October, 1959), 313–21.

[51] See William Barrett, *Irrational Man* (Garden City, N.Y., 1962), 270–71.

[52] *The Public Philosophy*, 124–25.

objectively, not subjectively. It can be discovered. It has to be obeyed." [53]

Second, the natural law also declares the value of the human person as a reasoning, self-conscious being. Man's worth rests on the fact that he is an "inviolable person," an "immortal soul," a "created entity." From this basic postulate essential political maxims can be legitimately derived.

Third, Lippmann's viewpoint does not pretend to set up a political ideal "complete with all the doors and windows in place and the house rules solidly and firmly established." [54] Rather, it recognizes the interaction of the two realms, of essence and existence, of abiding value and transient circumstance. Practical decisions are prudently made in the tension of the two realms as men, conscious of the pressing impingement of such spiritual values as love, charity, and compassion, employ wisdom to guard and develop the potentialities of personhood.

Fourth, Lippmann has not proposed anything which would sanctify the status quo. Neither does he desire to turn history back to any previously existent political or social system. All of men's schemes and systems are under the judgment of the realm of the spirit. Criticism and improvement are always in order.

Fifth, Lippmann is not advocating any artificial limits on human freedom. Instead, he is seeking recognition of the fact that human freedom *is* limited "in the nature of things," and that it is the task of politics to determine the viable limits on freedom in the name of community and order.

The Unfinished Pilgrimage

The political setting for Walter Lippmann's half-century pilgrimage involves a complex attempt to discover a stable basis for democratic government. The continuing question has been: "Why do democratic societies appear to lose vitality and decisiveness precisely during those periods in which they need most these qual-

[53] *Ibid.*, 133.
[54] Engberg, "Walter Lippmann's World," 170.

ities?" [55] As we have seen, his search for answers has lead him down many roads and countless byways. He has, at times, been preoccupied with institutional reforms; he has given himself to an analysis of public opinion; he has clarified the definition of the people's role in a liberal polity. Out of these and other diverse efforts and reflections has emerged his strong conviction that, before all else, there is need for an understanding in depth of human beings in political society. And out of the insights gained in his own attempts to achieve such an understanding, he has evolved the concept of the public philosophy.

The process has not been easy. Commenting on Arthur Schlesinger's essay in *Walter Lippmann and His Times*, Lippmann has written: "I have reread Arthur Schlesinger's assessment . . . I can say that his description of a long search and much turmoil is entirely plausible." [56] In this study the search has been termed a pilgrimage. The designation is not inappropriate. As a quest for enduring foundations for both the good life and the good society, the journey has led beyond the "multi-verse" of modern skepticism to the two-dimensional universe of essence and existence. The philosophy which has gripped him is contrary "not only to the fashion of the day, but to the entire movement of the epoch as well. It is contrary to the positivism, the nominalism, the materialism, and the nihilism that have held the universities of the West in thrall since the middle of the last century." [57]

The fruit of the pilgrimage includes certain preliminary propositions that are, it seems to me, almost impossible to refute. That constitutional democracy requires a public philosophy is constantly disputed today, even by some of democracy's most fervent supporters, but Lippmann's arguments remain convincing. Government in a democracy is government by consent, and government by consent cannot mean that each citizen consents to each law; this is a political absurdity. What it does mean is that all citizens, considered as a community, are voluntarily committed to a particular

[55] *Ibid.*, 168.
[56] Lippmann to Edward Engberg, November 7, 1961.
[57] Halle, "Walter Lippmann," 18.

style of government and, therefore, to a broad common understanding of and attitude toward law. The effective functioning of a democratic state is ultimately dependent upon such a consensus. That the United States is a pluralistic society cannot be denied. But it is not so radically pluralistic—at least, not yet—as to become segmented into isolated commonalties. Underneath the pattern of pluralization is a deep current of consensus, structuring the community and projecting the shape of the state. This consensus covers a multitude of political matters: nonarbitrary law, legal equality, civil liberties, personal worth, the maximization of freedom within order. Crisis and catastrophe may strain the fabric of political community to the utmost. Sections of the society may temporarily desert key portions of the democratic creed. But, so long as the foundational consensus endures in the minds and loyalties of the people, the fabric is likely to hold. Once the foundations have been eroded, however, no such assurance remains. Contemporary history vividly teaches this lesson.

As an example of the danger Lippmann sees so clearly, one can point to the contemporary problems of dissent and political alienation in the United States. The traumatic, sudden, violent demands of minority groups for social, political, and economic power have put serious strain on the ties cementing the country into a political entity. Whether the United States can finally emerge from such a crisis as a healthy, functioning, democratic organism actually depends upon the quality of the consensus which binds Americans together. Two aspects of the public philosophy are the foci of the problem: first, the meaning and implications of equality based on the absolute value of the human person; and second, government by law—defined as the use of nonarbitrary legal procedures to implement decisions arrived at by discussion, persuasion, and compromise. The first of these principles operates to validate the rights of all citizens to an equality of status and opportunity. The second requires that the necessary reshaping of the community structure finally take place along established, reasonable lines of democratic procedure; that there be reform, not revolution.

In the current crisis the two principles are often in tension with one another, with resultant strain. If the public philosophy still shapes and moderates the commitments of enough Americans, prudent paths toward progress, adjustment, and solution can be found. If, however, the foundations which sustain the public philosophy are insubstantial, an irrational conflict of personal, racial, and class interests will replace the liberal democratic process. In such an event, the only answer to the conflict is a resort to raw power. The most frightening aspect of the contemporary American situation is the appearance of unmistakable cracks in the working democratic consensus. Lippmann's judgment is that the foundations have already eroded; how far remains to be seen. The intellectual and spiritual atmosphere of modernity is hostile to any significant recognition of abiding, reasonable values and standards. The public world to which men still pay lip-service is shadowy and ineffective in relation to most political decisions. The one-dimensional horizon of many men forecloses any genuine confrontation with the realm of spiritual essence. And the failure to recognize the two realms and their implications for political life threatens finally to sink the ship of the public philosophy. Democracy, freedom, order, and personal integrity would be left to struggle in a sea of moral relativism, clinging desperately to the rotten timbers of traditional procedural norms. But political techniques will not long survive if they cannot stamp their legitimacy imperatively upon the minds and wills of men. They must possess "the signs and seals of legitimacy, of rightness and truth." They must have a "mandate from heaven." [58]

Does Lippmann's concept of the public philosophy carry with it such a mandate? To acknowledge the strength of his total case does not imply that there are not serious questions concerning the source and content of his philosophy. Most men will fail to be convinced by the overly pragmatic tendency in Lippmann which leads him sometimes to argue for natural law largely because the survival of the democratic way of life seems to require it. Such an argument may say a great deal about democracy, but it says little

[58] *The Public Philosophy*, 138.

about the independent validity of the public philosophy. Much more must be established if the skeptic is to find the proof compelling.

It can also be argued that Lippmann has failed to take account of the full resources of the "tradition of civility" to which he has so eloquently appealed. While it is not appropriate to judge Lippmann's concepts in terms of their consistency with faith-convictions which Lippmann himself does not accept, he has appealed to the historic Christian tradition as the most important bearer of the truths giving substance and power to the public philosophy. It is valid, therefore, to question whether Lippmann has accurately interpreted that tradition.

Nowhere in his writings has Lippmann set out any systematic body of doctrine or metaphysics. What he has done is to declare his belief in a kingdom of the spirit out of which, as men reason about the "nature of things," they may draw the postulates of a natural law. Though he contends that such a belief is an indispensable support for the progress of civilization, his argument for its reality is not simply utilitarian. He reasons that in every man there is, after all empirical judgments have been made, a residual essence—"something left over." The recognition of this inviolable core of human personality has constituted the center of the "traditions of civility." "Natural law is simply the law implicit in a world that exists to protect and cultivate this 'something left over which is the heart of the matter.' " [59]

When the Christian Gospel proclaims that man is a created and immortal soul, it is, Lippmann believes, certifying this truth of the value of the inviolable person. In terms of its own mythology it is reflecting and communicating the nature of the realm of essence. Because the influence of the Gospel in this respect has been steady and inexhaustible, it stands as the principle bulwark within the Western cultural tradition of the public philosophy.

From the theological standpoint Lippmann's entire analysis begins with and never actually breaks through the limits of his funda-

[59] Halle, "Walter Lippmann," 18.

mentally humanistic orientation. The realms of essence and existence are postulated on the basis of an introspective examination of
man's own postulated nature and experience. In an article endorsed by Lippmann, Edward Engberg has pointed out that Lippmann's purpose has always been to provide a viable substitute for
the "Great Fictions," including the traditional belief in a transcendent, supernatural God, in the life of man. In this sense God,
like the state and society, is regarded as an artificial construct
which, however, arises as the object of fundamental human desire. To seek to understand this desire and the reality of human
experience to which it corresponds is to engage in the search for a
realm of essence and for a natural law.[60]

That there is an objective reality of which these constructs are
the manifestation is Lippmann's declaration of faith. His humanistic orientation constrains him, however, so that he is extremely re-
luctant to venture beyond the bounds of immanence and introspection. He is willing to speak of man as a created soul, but he has
little to say—certainly not in any definitive sense—about the transcendent structure of reality out of which creation arises. His two-
dimensional concept of reality is not a two-story edifice which can
be simply equated with the historic Christian distinction between
the immanent and the transcendent. Instead it is a split-level
concept which never rises above the height of man's own nature. Within these limits Lippmann can speak only vaguely of a
doctrine of creation. Of the Christian doctrines of judgment and
redemption—certainly as central in the historic tradition as is
creation—he cannot really talk at all. Lippmann seems to have
grasped the significance of the Christian affirmation of an inde-
structible continuity between God and his creation, but he has
failed to do proper justice to the equally basic declaration of an
irreducible discontinuity between God and man. Perhaps the crux
of the problem is that Lippmann appears to retain far more faith
in the reliability of man's reason than do many contemporary
Christians. A strong segment of modern Christian thought centers
upon the contention that human sin creates a gap between man

[60] Engberg, "Walter Lippmann's World," 168–69.

and ultimate reality which affects the total human personality, including his reason.

How drastically man's ability to use his reason is affected by the infection of self-centeredness and the will to power is undoubtedly a debatable question. Yet, it would appear that Lippmann cannot have his cake and eat it, too. In other words, he cannot claim the support of the historic Christian tradition without coming to grips with the full sweep of that tradition. He does violence to the mainstream Christian proclamation when he interprets its central thrust as a simple doctrine of personal integrity based on man's creation in the image of God. No Christian declaration, for instance, of the inviolability of the person can be made on the basis of creation alone, for the harmonious pattern of creation is empirically marred and distorted by the existential reality of sin, suffering, and evil. The evidence of men's inequality, weakness, and wickedness is too forceful, too painful, to be overcome by a doctrine of creation—especially one which, like Lippmann's, is earthbound.

The Christian Gospel loses its power to reflect reality with accuracy unless the doctrines of judgment and redemption are placed alongside the teaching of creation. Judgment declares not only that there are absolute standards, drawn from a realm of essence, but also that each individual person is obligated by, responsible to, and condemned by that fixed moral order. Without a sense of judgment, it is doubtful that men take sin with due seriousness, even when they do not deny the obvious evidences of evil. "Modern man has an essentially easy conscience; and nothing gives the diverse and discordant notes of modern culture so much harmony as the unanimous opposition of modern man to Christian conceptions of the sinfulness of man." [61] Lippmann sees as clearly as any modern observer that modern man's "easy conscience" is a pretense which hides the pervasive spread of anguish and despair,[62] but he fails to follow up this insight into man's predica-

[61] Reinhold Niebuhr, *The Nature and Destiny of Man* (2 vols.; New York, 1941), vol. I, 131
[62] See *The Public Philosophy*, 84–87

ment. It is the doctrine of judgment which interprets the true reality of human guilt, the actual dimensions of human freedom, and the integral responsibility of every man.

Christian doctrine had also traditionally asserted that it is the understanding of redemption which gives genuine support to the inviolable value of the person. Its declaration substitutes for Lippmann's "something left over" an objective divine demonstration of man's worth, divorced finally from any empirical or subjective analysis of value. Sin is seen, not as the inevitable consequence of man's human finiteness or as the inescapable result of his involvement in the contingencies of existence, but as rebellion against the Creator and Governor of the universe. The alienation and discontinuity resulting from sin is perceived as being more complex than a conflict between man's two natures. Essential man cannot be extricated from nonessential man. The rebellion of man involves his total nature, and no part of human personality, such as reason, can be divorced from judgment. Since sin arises out of man's will to act or to reason in particular ways, it permeates every part of man's nature. In the light of this observation, it becomes essential to maintain that men possess value, not because of any original act of creation, viewed in isolation, but because their alienation from the Creator has been overcome by an objective act of reconciliation, arising out of the transcendent source of reality. This is the claim of Christianity. The value of a human being is conferred by a redemptive act originating in ultimate Being. This redemptive reality gives to every man infinite value as a person, not as a thing.

I find myself ready to agree with Lippmann that the Christian faith has carried the major weight of the public philosophy in Western civilization. I am convinced by his arguments for the indispensable function of this philosophy in the patterns of a liberal society. But I would argue that Lippmann has failed to draw upon the full strength of the Christian proclamation. The strength of the Gospel is not alone in a doctrine of creation and "residual essence" but in the total declaration of the meaning and implications of creation, judgment, and redemption. And one can rightly question whether an argument which ignores the correspondence of this full proclamation to the essential and existential realities of life can finally validate and legitimize the public philosophy.

Lippmann's understanding of the human problem commands deep respect. It is rooted in a significant faith in the relevance of a moral universe and realm of absolutes. There are exciting indications that the directions of his development—the path of his pilgrimage—could uncover new dimensions in the historic natural law tradition. His work constitutes a major effort by a man of light and learning to speak to his contemporaries about ultimate issues.

At the present stage in his pilgrimage, however, Lippmann's underlying affirmation remains one of faith in man, rather than in God. He is committed to the worth and dignity of all human beings. He is committed to the hope that the best human minds, using a broad and classic reason, sensitive to the historic experience of mankind, may in the process of time convincingly lay bare the structure of ultimate reality. Some fundamentally important things are already clear about that structure, and by these truths men of integrity are obligated to live. Much remains to be discovered. The struggle to discover is the inescapable heritage of any man who is willing to think. The quest constitutes the challenge which makes the human story an adventure and the human endeavor worthwhile. Walter Lippmann has invested much of his life and talent in that quest.

The pilgrimage continues.

Bibliography

SELECTED WORKS OF WALTER LIPPMANN

Books

Editor. *The Poems of Paul Mariett.* New York, 1913.
A Preface to Politics. New York, 1913.
Drift and Mastery. New York, 1914.
The Stakes of Diplomacy. New York, 1915.
Liberty and the News. New York, 1920.
Public Opinion. New York, 1922.
The Phantom Public. New York, 1925.
Men of Destiny. New York, 1927.
American Inquisitors. New York, 1928.
A Preface to Morals. New York, 1929.
Interpretations, 1931–1932. Ed. Allan Nevins. New York, 1933.
The Method of Freedom. New York, 1934.
The New Imperative. New York, 1935.
Interpretations, 1933–1935. Ed. Allan Nevins. New York, 1936.
The Good Society. New York, 1937.
U.S. Foreign Policy: Shield of the Republic. Boston, 1943.
U.S. War Aims. Boston, 1944.
The Cold War. New York, 1947.
The Public Philosophy. New York, 1955.
The Communist World and Ours. Boston, 1958.

186

The Coming Tests with Russia. Boston, 1961.
Western Unity and the Common Market. Boston, 1962.
The Essential Lippmann. Ed. Clinton Rossiter and James Lare. New York, 1963.

Articles

"In Defense of the Suffragettes," *Harvard Monthly,* XLIX (November, 1909), 64–67.
"Harvard in Politics: A Problem in Imperceptibles," *Harvard Monthly,* XLIX (December, 1909), 95–98.
"An Open Mind: William James," *Everybody's Magazine,* XXIII (December, 1910), 800–801.
"Two Months in Schenectady," *The Masses,* III (April, 1912), 13.
"The Most Dangerous Man in the World," *Everybody's Magazine,* XXVII (July, 1912), 100–101.
"The Vocabulary of Political Thought," *New Republic,* IV (August 7, 1915), 24.
"Uneasy America," *New Republic,* V (December 25, 1915), 334–35.
"An Epic of Desire," *New Republic,* VII (May 6, 1916), 21–22.
"The Hope of Democracy," *New Republic,* VII (July 1, 1916), 231.
"The Case for Wilson," *New Republic,* VIII (October 14, 1916), 263–64.
"The Basic Problem of Democracy," *Atlantic Monthly,* CXXIV (November, 1919), 616–27.
"Unrest," *New Republic,* XX (November 12, 1919), 315–22.
"Second-Hand Statesmen," *Yale Review,* n. s. XI (July, 1922), 673–86.
"A Defense of Education," *Century,* CVI (May, 1923), 95–103.
"Why Should the Majority Rule?" *Harper's,* CLII (March, 1926), 399–405.
"Autocracy Versus Catholicism," *Commonweal,* V (April 13, 1927), 527.
"Humanism as Dogma," *Saturday Review of Literature,* VI (March 15, 1930), 817–19.
"Free Time and Extra Money," *Woman's Home Companion,* LVII (April, 1930), 31–32.
"Notes for a Biography," *New Republic,* LXIII (July 16, 1930), 250–52.
"The Scholar in a Troubled World," *Atlantic Monthly,* CL (August, 1932), 148–52.
"In Defense of Liberalism," *Vanity Fair,* XLIII (November, 1934), 24.
"Challenge to the Constitution," *American Magazine,* CXIX (June, 1935), 44–45ff.

"A Tribute to Theodore Roosevelt, October 27, 1858–1935," *Woman's Roosevelt Memorial Association*, 1935.

"The Living Organism of Our Society," *Vital Speeches of the Day*, II (December 30, 1935), 186–88.

"The Deepest Issue of Our Time," *Vital Speeches of the Day*, II (July 1, 1936), 602–604.

Address at William and Mary College, New York *Herald-Tribune* (April 24, 1937), 17.

"Loud-Mouthed Barbarians," *Vital Speeches of the Day*, III (July 15, 1937), 387–89.

Address to Salvation Army Dinner, New York, New York *Herald-Tribune* (March 23, 1938), 21.

"National Defense Through Patriotic Education," *National Defense News*, III (April-May, 1939), 8–11.

"The Indispensable Opposition," *Atlantic Monthly*, CLXIV (August, 1939), 186–90.

"The State of Education in this Troubled Age," *Vital Speeches of the Day*, VII (January 15, 1941), 200–203.

"Man's Image of Man," *Commonweal*, XXXV (February 13, 1942), 406–409.

"On the Unity of Mankind," *Rotarian*, LXXI (October, 1947), 9–12.

"A Rejoinder," *Yale Review*, n.s. XLIV (June, 1955), 497–500.

SECONDARY SOURCES CITED

Books

Arendt, Hannah. *The Origins of Totalitarianism*. New York, 1961.

Aristotle. *Nichomachean Ethics*. Trans. W. D. Ross. In *Great Books of the Western World*. Ed. Robert M. Hutchins. 54 vols. Chicago, 1952. Vol. IX, 339–444.

Barker, Ernest. *Principles of Social and Political Theory*. Oxford, 1951.

———. *Traditions of Civility*. Cambridge, 1948.

Barrett, William. *Irrational Man*. Garden City, N.Y., 1962.

Berle, Adolf A., Jr. and Gardiner C. Means. *The Modern Corporation and Private Property*. New York, 1937.

Brown, John Mason. *Through These Men*. New York, 1956.

Bryce, James B. *Modern Democracies*. 2 vols. New York, 1921.

Cassirer, Ernest. *The Myth of the State*. New Haven, 1946.

Childs, Marquis and James Reston (eds.). *Walter Lippmann and His Times*. New York, 1959.

d'Entrèves, A. P. *Natural Law*. London, 1951.

Durkheim, Emile. *Suicide*. Trans. John A. Spaulding and George Simpson. 2 vols. Glencoe, Ill., 1951.

Forcey, Charles B. *The Crossroads of Liberalism*. New York, 1961.

Frankel, Charles. *The Democratic Prospect*. New York and Evanston, 1961.

Gierke, Otto. *Political Theories of the Middle Ages*. Trans. F. W. Maitland. Cambridge, 1900.

——. *Natural Law and the Theory of Society*. Trans. Ernest Barker. Boston, 1957.

Grant, F. C. *Hellenistic Religions: The Age of Syncretism*. New York, 1953.

Hallowell, John H. *The Moral Foundation of Democracy*. Chicago, 1954.

Hart, H. L. A. *The Concept of Law*. Oxford, 1961.

Hicks, Granville. *John Reed*. New York, 1936.

Holmes, Oliver Wendell. *Collected Papers*. New York, 1920.

Howe, Mark DeWolfe (ed.). *The Holmes–Laski Letters*. 2 vols. Cambridge, Mass., 1953.

James, William. *The Meaning of Truth*. New York, 1909.

——. *Pragmatism*. New York, 1929.

Kelsen, Hans. *General Theory of Law and State*. Trans. Anders Wedberg. Cambridge, Mass., 1945.

Lindeman, E. C. *Social Discovery*. Introduction by Herbert Croly. New York, 1926.

Llewellyn, Karl N. *The Bramble Bush*. New York, 1951.

Lovett, Robert Morss. *All Our Years*. New York, 1948.

Luhan, Mabel Dodge. *Movers and Shakers*. New York, 1936.

Morison, Samuel Eliot. *Three Centuries at Harvard, 1636–1936*. Cambridge, Mass., 1936.

Murray, John Courtney. *We Hold These Truths*. New York, 1960.

Niebuhr, Reinhold. *The Nature and Destiny of Man*. 2 vols. New York, 1941.

Ortega y Gassett, José. *The Revolt of the Masses*. Authorized translation from the Spanish. New York, 1932.

Ramsey, Paul. *Nine Modern Moralists*. Englewood Cliffs, N.J., 1962.

Reed, John. *The Day in Bohemia*. New York, 1913.

Riesman, David. *The Lonely Crowd*. New Haven, 1950.

Russell, Bertrand. *A History of Western Philosophy*. New York, 1945.

Santayana, George. *Character and Opinion in the United States*. New York, 1920.

——. *The Life of Reason*. 5 vols. New York, 1962.

Schilpp, Paul Arthur (ed.). *The Philosophy of George Santayana*. Evanston and Chicago, 1940.

Shotwell, James T. *At the Paris Peace Conference.* New York, 1937.

Smith, John. *Select Discourses.* 4th ed. Cambridge, 1859.

Sorel, Georges. *Reflections on Violence.* Trans. T. E. Hulme and J. Roth. Glencoe, Ill., 1950.

Spitz, David. *Democracy and the Challenge of Power.* New York, 1958.

————. *Patterns of Anti-Democratic Thought.* New York, 1949.

Steffens, Lincoln. *Autobiography.* New York, 1931.

Tillich, Paul. *Systematic Theology.* 3 vols. Chicago, 1951–63.

Toynbee, Arnold. *A Study of History.* 12 vols. London, 1934–61.

Voegelin, Eric. *The New Science of Politics.* Chicago, 1952.

————. *Order and History.* 3 vols. Baton Rouge, 1957.

Wallas, Graham. *Human Nature in Politics.* 3rd ed. New York, 1921.

Ways, Max. *Beyond Survival.* New York, 1959.

Weingast, David E. *Walter Lippmann.* New Brunswick, N.J., 1949.

White, Morton. *Social Thought in America: The Revolt Against Formalism.* 2nd ed. Boston, 1957.

Willey, Basil. *The Seventeenth Century Background.* New York, 1934.

Articles

Baker, Newton D. "The Good Society of the Future," *Atlantic Monthly,* CLX (November, 1937), 612–16.

Bates, Ernest Sutherland. "Walter Lippmann: The Career of Comrade Fool," *Modern Monthly,* VII (June, 1933), 266–74.

Cain, James M. "The End of the World," *New Freeman,* II (March 11, 1931), 610–12.

Dinkler, E. "Myth," in *The Interpreter's Dictionary of the Bible,* ed. G. A. Buttrick. 4 vols. New York, 1962, Vol. K–Q, 487.

Engberg, Edward. "Walter Lippmann's World," *Commonweal,* LXXV (November 10, 1961), 167–70.

Eulau, Heinz. "From Public Opinion to Public Philosophy," *American Journal of Economics and Sociology,* XV (July, 1956), 439–51.

Flynn, John. "Other People's Money," *New Republic,* LXXXVIII (September 23, 1936), 183–84.

Forcey, Charles B. "Leadership and 'Misrule by the People'," *New Republic,* CXXXII (February 21, 1955), 13–16.

Giles, Barbara. "Pundit in a Penthouse," *New Masses,* XXXVI (September 10, 1940), 11–12.

Halle, Louis J. "Walter Lippmann," *New Republic,* CXLIX (August 3, 1963), 19–20.

Handlin, Oscar. "Does the People's Rule Doom Democracy?" *Commentary,* XX (July, 1955), 1–8.

Hook, Sidney. "Do the People Rule and Can They?" *New York Times Book Review*, July 14, 1963, 1ff.

Jones, Ernest. Review of Walter Lippmann's *A Preface to Politics*. *Imago* (Vienna), II (no. 4, 1913), 452–56.

Kuklis, Robert D. "The Democratic Faith of a Young Intellectual." Typescript in Lippmann Collection, Yale University.

Lasswell, Harold D. Review of Walter Lippmann's *The Phantom Public*, in *American Journal of Sociology*, XXXI (January, 1926), 533–35.

MacLeish, Archibald. "The Alternative," *Yale Review*, n.s. XLIV (June, 1955), 481–96.

McIlwain, C. H. "Government by Law," *Foreign Affairs*, XIV (January, 1936), 185–98.

Marshall, Margaret. "Columnists on Parade," *Nation*, CXLVI (April 23, 1938), 464–67.

Matthews, Shailer. "The Religious Basis of Ethics," *Journal of Religion*, X (April, 1930), 222–31.

Mercier, L. J. A. "Columnists and Professors," *Commonweal*, XXXI (January 26, 1940), 296–98.

———. "Walter Lippmann's Evolution," *Commonweal*, XXX (August 4, 1939), 348–50.

Morgenthau, Hans J. "Reason and Restoration in the West," *New Republic*, CXXXII (February 21, 1956), 12–13ff.

Morrow, Felix. "Religion and the Good Life," *The Menorah Journal*, XVIII (February, 1930), 99–117.

Muller, William D. "An Interpretation of the Political Philosophy of Walter Lippmann: The Nature of Man." Typescript in Lippmann Collection, Yale University.

Noble, David W. "The *New Republic* and the Idea of Progress, 1914–20," *Mississippi Valley Historical Review*, XXXVIII (December, 1951), 387–402.

Phillips, David C. "Walter Lippmann and the New Philosophies, 1910–1935." Unpublished honors paper, Williams College, 1958. Typescript in Lippmann Collection, Yale University.

Pinchot, Amos. "Walter Lippmann: I. The Great Elucidator," *Nation*, CXXXVII (July 5, 1933), 7–10.

Rubenstein, Annette T. "Disinterestedness as Ideal and Technique," *Journal of Philosophy*, XXVIII (August 13, 1931), 461–66.

Schutz, Charles E. "The Development and Significance of the Political Thought of Walter Lippmann," Ph.D. dissertation, University of Chicago, 1962.

Smith, Warren Allen. "Authors and Humanism," *The Humanist*, XI (October, 1941), 193–204.

"Spiritual Revolution," *Commonweal*, XXIII (March 13, 1936), 533–34.

Spitz, David. "Freedom, Virtue, and the New Scholasticism," *Commentary*, XXVIII (October, 1959), 313–21.

Underwood, Frank H. Review of Walter Lippmann's *The Public Philosophy*, in *Canadian Forum*, XXXIV (March, 1955), 284–85.

Wilson, Edmond. "Antidote to Despair," *New Republic*, LIX (July 10, 1929), 210–11.

Index

Absolutes: incompatibility with pluralism, 125; and public philosophy, 150; imitation, 155; attempted easy application of, 156; conceptual, 166
Acton, Lord, 169
Addams, Jane, 61
Aestheticism: Santayana on, 14n, 16, 36; Lippmann and, 56
Agnosticism, 162
Albertson, Fay (wife of Lippmann), 19
Albertson, Ralph (father-in-law of Lippmann), 19
Altizer, Thomas J. J., 146n
Apollo Belvedere, 51
Aquinas, Thomas: political theory of, 3–4; and natural law, 115, 116, 160, 165; mentioned, 134, 166
Aristotle: and Lippmann's humanism, 37; on citizenship, 91; and prudence, 157; quoted by Lippmann, 158
Arnold, Matthew, 111
Atheism, 133
Augustine, St., 3
Authority: in higher law, 37; dangers in, 63; democracy and, 81; in law, 108; human nature and, 111, 127; incredibility of religious, 128
Autonomy of man, 111, 149

Baker, George Pierce, 12
Baker, Newton D., 30
Beauty, 169
Bentham, Jeremy, 92
Bergson, Henry: influence on Lippmann, 15, 36, 47; Lippmann's criticism of, 19–20, 26; on intuitiveness, 53; mentioned, 23, 25
Bible, The, 158
Blackstone, William, 118
Bodin, Jean, 102
Boston *Common*, 19
Bryan, William Jennings, 76–78 *passim*
Bryce, James, 72
Buddha, Gautama, 77
Bull Moose Party. *See* Progressive Party
Bunyan, John, 148
Burke, Edmund, 41, 91

Cain, James M., 9
Cambridge Platonists, 142–43
Casuistry, 156
Catholic Church: and natural law, 115; as block to progress, 124; Lippmann's reported affiliation with, 134
Chicago Vice Commission, 97–99 *passim*
Christian Gospel: and human nature, 120; Lippmann's attitude toward, 144; historicity of, 145–46; and religious modernism, 145; and abstract truths, 150
Christianity: contribution to "good society," 42; Lippmann and, 122–23, 134, 181; as block to progress, 124; and human value, 132, 184; as myth, 138, 139; effectiveness of, 145; and freedom, 147
Churches: and higher law, 50; Lippmann's views of, 123, 124, 126, 128, 129; and totalitarianism, 130
Churchill, Winston, 10, 43
Cicero, 160
Citizen: omnicompetence of, 151; role of, 152. *See also* People
Civic Service House (Boston), 17
Civilization: and disinterested man, 58–59; survival of, 70, 119; and law, 107–108, 118–19; needs of, 119
Cobb, Frank, 31, 33
Coercion. *See* Power
Coke, Sir Edward, 108
Cold War, 173–74
Collectivism: Lippmann's analysis of, 39, 63, 89; and liberalism, 40, 89; rise of, 107; religion and, 130, 131
Communication: role of elite in, 55; and news distortion, 86; role of in society, 112
Communism: Lippmann's attitude toward, 20, 22, 39; and value systems, 165
Community: man and, 59, 149; Bentham's definition of, 92; and history, 92; popular will as enemy of, 152
Compromise, 173, 173n
Confucius, 3, 37

193